PENNY ARCADE™

PENNY–ARCADE.COM

BY JERRY HOLKINS & MIKE KRAHULIK

dark horse books™

Publisher
MIKE RICHARDSON

Editor
MIKE CARRIGLITTO

Designer
DAVID NESTELLE

Art Director
LIA RIBACCHI

PENNY ARCADE Volume 1: ATTACK OF THE BACON ROBOTS!

This volume collects comic strips from the Penny Arcade website, originally published online from November 18, 1998 through December 29, 2000.

Published by
Dark Horse Books
A division of Dark Horse Comics, Inc.
10956 SE Main Street
Milwaukie, OR 97222

darkhorse.com

To find a comics shop in your area, call the Comic Shop Locator Service toll-free at 1-888-266-4226

First edition: January 2006
ISBN: 1-59307-444-1

10 9 8 7 6 5 4 3
Printed in China

Foreword by Bill Amend

 was a little surprised when the Penny Arcade guys invited me to write this introduction.

Yes, I do a comic strip, and yes, *FoxTrot* has an abundance of computer and video game jokes, but the similarities really end there. Let's be honest: my strip is but a Pat Boone to their Metallica. Or more aptly, a Yoshi to their Diablo.

Penny Arcade channels some sort of raw, unfiltered gamer id in ways that are not for everyone. The Web is the unsupervised wild west of cartooning, and these boys are running around with BFGs. If you are easily upset by gore, four-letter words, sacrilege, juvenile wang jokes, or don't know what a BFG is, do yourself a favor and put this book down before you wind up rinsing your eyeballs with Clorox. If you're unsure, at least have a bottle ready to go in the cupboard. Still with me? Well, you were warned.

One of the things I really like about *Penny Arcade* is how normal it makes me feel. I used to think I had a video game "problem." I used to think my routinely staying up past 3:00 A.M. on a work night typing "gg" to strangers with names like DETHANGEL007 and FRAGLORD was somehow, well, weird. Au contraire, I've discovered. In fact, based on what I've gleaned from *PA*, my gaming tendencies are more on the "dabbler" end of the spectrum.

Once upon a time, back before I reallocated my talent points, I was pretty good at math. I was a physics major in college. Yet, for the life of me, I can't see how Mike and Jerry do what they do. There just aren't enough hours in the day to play all the games they talk about. Computer games.

Console games. Handheld games. I believe I've even seen a D20 show up a couple times. And they still have time left over to do a strip. And write all kinds of commentary on their Web site. And it's not crap. It's really good. In fact, often the art alone looks like it took days and days to do. All I can figure is they've discovered how to warp the fabric of time in ways that I can't. I want my parents' tuition money back.

Those of us who do newspaper strips have to serve many masters. We have to do a strip that our syndicate editors like, that newspaper editors like, and that a large number of their readers like if we hope to be published for more than a week. Because of this, we tend toward more general subjects like golf and swimsuits and our humor necessarily resides in the "family-friendly" realm. Web cartoonists, however, get to play by different rules. Some stay close to what's worked in papers, others just do whatever they want. *Penny Arcade*, with its no-holds-barred views and oftentimes insanely obscure references, definitely falls into the latter camp. One always gets the sense that these two are writing and drawing things born of pure personal expression. Good or bad. For the sheer fun of it. That they've created the most popular comic on the Web seems no more than a happy accident. In this bottom-line-driven, focus-grouped corporate media conglomerate world, it's heartening to see creative popularity soar on its own. Even if they did misspell "Aiur" once.

GJ guys.

—*Bill Amend*

Terribly Serious Introduction

*I*t's really strange. I've been writing *Penny Arcade* for coming up on seven years, no problems to speak of, but now that I'm writing something that will be printed in a book, I'm completely terrified. Try to explain that.

The premise and execution of *Penny Arcade* is such that, if you obtained this book by any means, you are probably already familiar with whatever it is we do. One does not simply enter a store to procure a highly obscure tome on a subject of no interest to them, unless they need to write a paper.

Let's pause for a moment and savor the notion of a universe where *Penny Arcade* has somehow become *required reading*.

Since it will be true in the highest percentage of cases, let me thank you, the longsuffering reader. Gabriel and I have discussed it, and we think you are great. It took five years of legal exertion to print the sentence you are reading, and, though we could never discuss the particulars of that nightmare, we were ever buoyed by your enthusiasm.

If you aren't familiar with *Penny Arcade*, it's probably best to think of the book you are holding in a purely anthropological sense: the dreams of a culture alien to you, somehow coalesced. Imagine that you have removed dust from the cover with a dry cloth, a team of scientists huddled behind you, all of them terribly curious about its contents.

—*Tycho Brahe*
August 3rd, 2005
Seattle, WA

Well, That Was Very Serious, Wasn't It?

Introductions are a form of writing that I don't really get to indulge in with any frequency—it's not like we put out a new book every fucking week. There was a lot of grim language there, not to mention factual inaccuracies: I've only been buoyed once in my entire life, and the time in question involved an actual buoy.

The thing at the end, though—with the name and the date? I mean, check me out. That's the kind of thing you would find in a real book, written by a real boy.

I said before that those unfamiliar with *Penny Arcade* should consider this book in a largely scientific context, but to a certain extent that is probably true for anyone who picks it up. As the Internet reckons time, they're practically artifacts. Indeed, we may even have used the now reviled .gif format. They're transmissions from a radically different era of personal publishing. These days, saying something offensive to the entire world is a turn-key enterprise. Even your mother may, on occasion, blog. In those heady days, the ones before the well publicized blogmom phenomenon, one felt as though they were engaging in a form of black magic.

Contrast that with today, where even as I'm writing for a book—which you'll recall is a solid, physical object—I just expect the ability to link any word I write to any other piece of writing, anywhere. I've already done it twice without meaning to. Must be some of that "progress" I keep hearing about.

The strips you'll soon be exposed to, and I am referring to them as I would a pathogen on purpose, represent the accidental genesis of a project that has come to consume our entire lives.

The exact origins of the site are somewhat nebulous. Sometimes I have dreams that might be memories, though—the two of us shattering the Repton blockade in a Usurper class broadwing. A universe collapsing inward, birthing an altogether new kind of energy. Strange, unyielding fields of gravity, their subatomic rhumba subtle and astonishing.

The truth of it is almost more nonsensical: we entered a cartooning contest and did not win. That's not positive stimuli. In fact, it probably should have ended it right there.

We went on to create the comics you see in this book. As you'll find, they're of all different sizes, created virtually at random. We had absolutely no idea what we were doing. If we succeeded at all, we can't take the credit.

THE SIN OF LONG LOAD TIMES

November 18, 1998 I haven't been through the archive in a while, so I'm basically reading through these, um, "Classics" with you. And I'm glad you're here, because I may need to be held from time to time. I really must tell you that when we uploaded comics like these, we felt like Goddamn emperors—at the time, it was rare for a webcomic to be in *color*. The "psychic ability" strip I'm less ashamed of than most—even now; I feel like it sets up the basic tones.

JOHN ROMERO: ARTISTE

November 25, 1998 This hot dog thing, though. Man, who fucking *knows*?

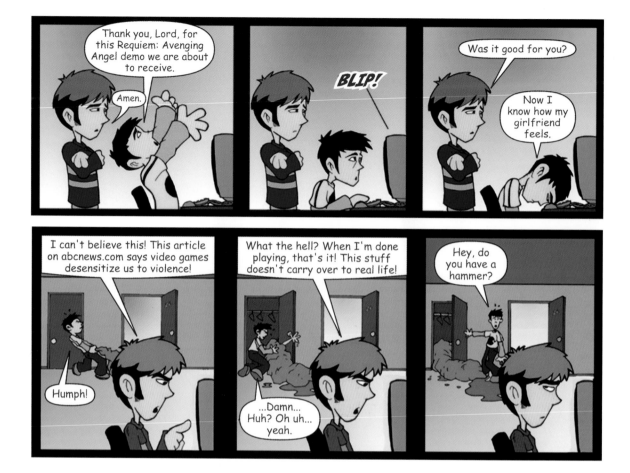

REQUIEM AA STRIP

December 2, 1998 Broadband might not be ubiquitous now, but most people have at least *heard* of it. The Requiem demo offered two or three minutes of gameplay for a hundred megabytes of download, which in 1998 was an almost inexpressible amount of data. It would be something like jamming a straw in the permafrost and trying to suck up Alaska.

VIDEO VIOLENCE

December 9, 1998 Before I came back through the archive, I wasn't aware that we had been touching on the (non)issue of violent gamers so early in our "career," such as it is. These days, our approach is somewhat more, uh . . . *nuanced*.

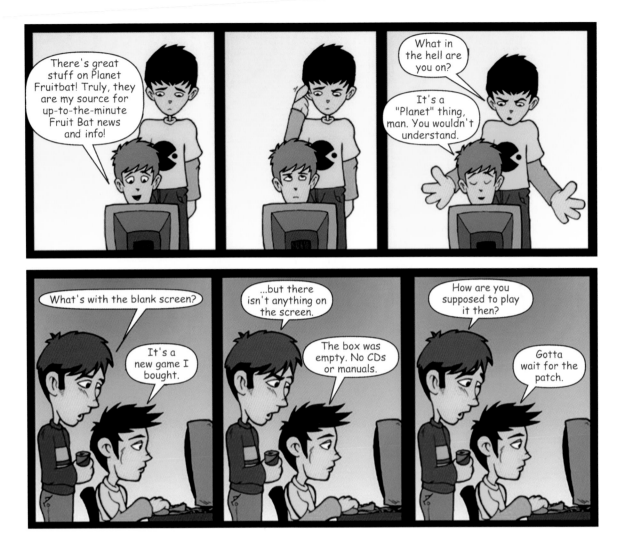

PLANET PROLIFERATION

December 16, 1998 Yes, well, I don't understand it either, cartoon, and I *wrote* you. This comic was created well before there was any such thing as a news post to accompany it. We'd just set a comic like this in front of a reader, grunt, and be on our way.

THE PATCH PARADE

December 21, 1998 The other comic on this page, "The Patch Parade," was created even before there *was* such a thing as *Penny Arcade*. It's one of the comics we made for that contest I mentioned earlier. I guess Gabe's shirt used to have a black stripe? We're learning these things *together*.

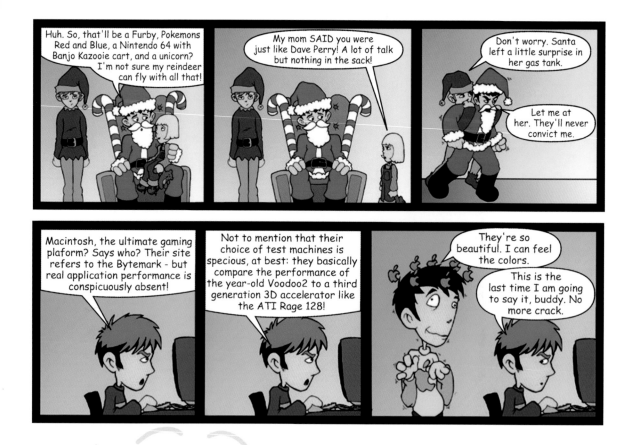

SHINY'S DAVE PERRY

December 23, 1998 I can remember that we were mad about something, something . . . to do . . . with games? Then Santa got involved? And then we killed a child. It's great that we're printing all these out, I'm sure they'll make a great Exhibit A in Huge Law Firm vs. My Stupid Ass.

MAC GAMING STRIP

January 13, 1999 Something else that characterized earlier *Penny Arcade* was hostility towards the Macintosh platform. Eventually we reached an accord with Mac users. There is a picture of us shaking hands at a somber ceremony.

MYTH II UNINSTALL

January 6, 1999 Yes, I'm aware that Bungie made Halo, but our favorite games from them were always prefaced by the word "Myth." An unorthodox real-time strategy game with an engaging universe and unmatched multiplayer, the sequel had a bug that could "uninstall" your Windows directory.

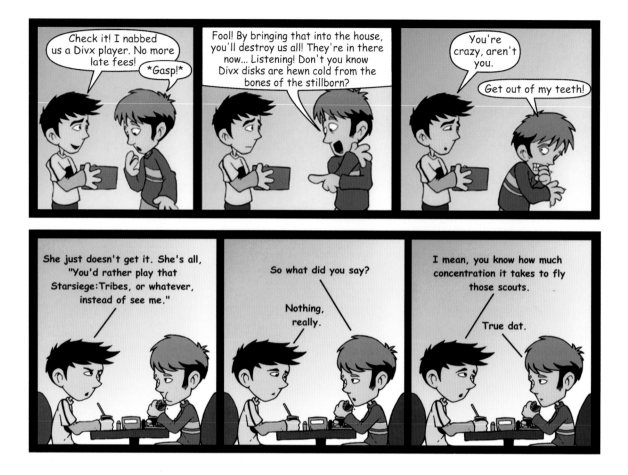

DIVX KILLS

January 15, 1999 An odd bit of trivia, here: there was a competitor to DVD called "Divx." It's hard to imagine, but essentially you could buy a movie for something like five bucks. You could watch it for a set amount of time, or pay *more* money to unlock it. It's not around anymore, I guess selling people movies they couldn't really own didn't quite work out.

GIRLFRIENDS, TRIBES, AND YOU

January 20, 1999 To this day, this strip will come up when we meet a long time reader. I guess we did something right? It is always my first instinct to say, "You liked that one? Well, you know, we did make *more . . .*"

SAVING PRIVATE ION

January 22, 1999 ION Storm was an odd phenomenon, a game designer supergroup like New Kids on the Block. The word on the street was that their office was a kind of Babylonian palace, where foreign birds nested and spigots flowed with exotic liquors. I can see having a spigot or two, fine, but that bird thing is ostentatious.

BALDURDASH

January 27, 1999 Only now—after smashing his face into the turn-based games *over* and *over*—does Gabriel understand how an hour of meticulous planning can deliver a satisfaction payload rivaling any genre. In fact, I think he probably spends more time with them than I do these days.

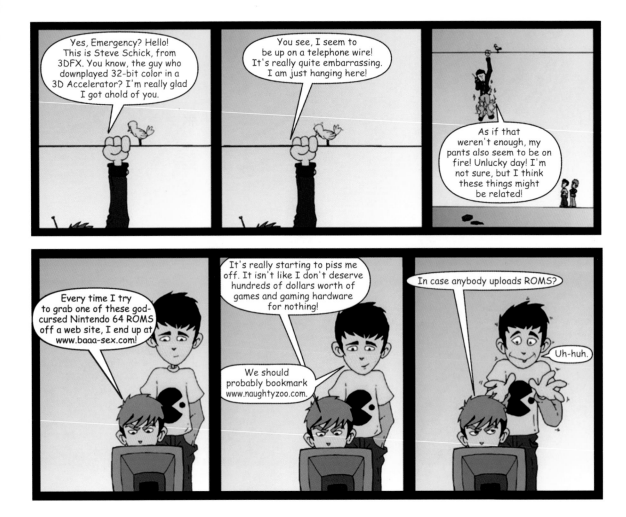

HANGIN' WITH 3DFX

January 29, 1999 And yeah, maybe 3dfx lied or whatever, but you can't really speak ill of the dead. After competitor nVidia gutted them and then held their spinal column aloft in some bizarre corporate ritual, I think they can probably be forgiven for the occasional exaggeration.

THE SEXY SIDE OF EMULATION

February 3, 1999 Please don't try to go to either of those URLs—they weren't real when we did the comic, and honestly I'm too scared to check if they've been put to some dark purpose. I'm confident that those who seek ROMs still walk through the valley of the shadow of *porn.*

THRASHIN' THRESH

February 5, 1999 As for Thresh, I mean, I don't know what he's doing these days. Probably beating the stems and husks of grain or cereal plants with a machine or flail to separate the seeds from the straw.

There's the cat, though. His name is Thomas Kemper, but it rarely comes up.

A BLOODY BIRTHDAY

February 10, 1999 Goddamn if the original Blood didn't have its claws in us deep. It utilized the old Build engine, made famous with "Duke Nukem 3D," sometimes called "Duke Nukem 2D." It had a terribly compelling mythology for a shooter, better than was strictly necessary. The sequel, as you might have detected, did not live up to it.

LET'S PLAY PRETEND!

February 12, 1999 This comic was the most elaborate thing we'd ever done to date, and it was so large that we originally sliced it into three separate images to ease digestion for modem-bound readers. We were hook, hook, *hooked* on the original Tribes, a first-person shooter that never felt beholden to the genre—or, indeed, the *ground*.

A little over two years ago I was standing in line for the re-release of *Star Wars* along with about half the country. My foresight had managed to secure me an enviable position at the head of an absurdly long line. It was hours before the box office was scheduled to open and the freezing temperatures did little to ease the long wait. I can remember the details of this day clearly for one reason. It wasn't because I was excited to see my favorite movie on the big screen for the first time. No, it was because it was on that day, in that line, that I met her. Now I had seen her before at work. No, that's not quite right, I had watched her before at work. However, it wasn't until *Star Wars* that we really connected on any kind of personal level. She recognized me from work and was obviously excited by my position in line. She asked if I would mind saving a seat for her. Well of course I didn't and that simple gesture began what has turned into an amazing two-year relationship.

As an artist I have been convinced of the inadequacies of the written language when it comes to the description of feelings or emotions for quite a while. However, there are times when you simply must say something when the creation of art is either not convenient or practical. So it is with a heavy heart that I am forced to express the feelings that I have for this girl, because I know that these emotions are poorly served by the simple words I must use. It is not enough for me to say that I love her. I have used this same word to describe my relationship with milk, my television, and those little bagel things with the pizza inside. So, to use it to describe the immense feelings and emotions that she elicits in me seems wrong. However, because I am an artist and not a writer I have no other words available to me at this time. So I will use it under the condition that anyone reading this knows that the word "love" is a mere shadow of the feeling I have for her. That no matter how beautiful it might be it is still only a shadow. The feeling itself, that which casts the shadow, is more brilliant and colorful than you can possibly imagine. With that said I suppose it is safe to continue.

I love you, Kara O'Donnal.
Will you please marry me?

A VERY SPECIAL PENNY ARCADE!

February 17, 1999 I remember coming back to the apartment after this went up, seeing Kara get out of Gabe's computer chair, look at me, smile, and wipe tears out of her eyes. I didn't remember that until just now.

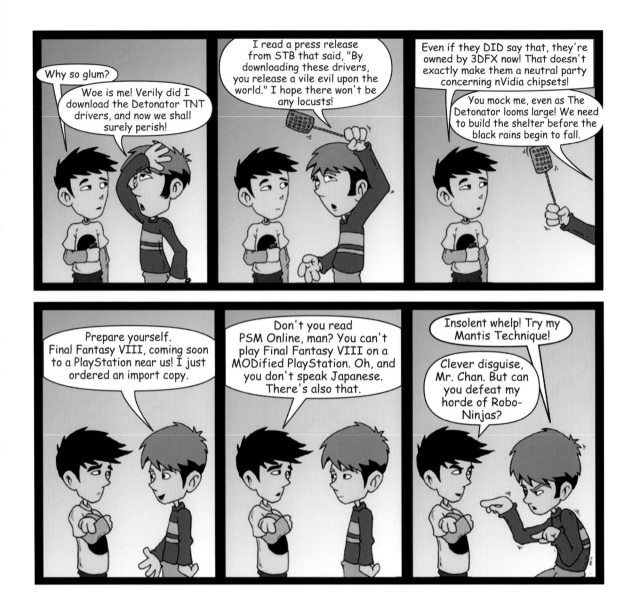

BEWARE THE DETONATOR

February 19, 1999 Bullshit of the "video card wars" variety hasn't gone anywhere. In fact, it's gotten *much worse*. It's strange to buy a game and have it tell me straight out that I own the wrong fucking card. Most recently, it had to do with ATI's almost *supernaturally* better performance on Valve's Source engine. And so it goes.

MANTIS STYLE AND MOD CHIPS

February 24, 1999 On the Mantis strip, for some reason I think that last panel was originally from another comic. If you can explain it how that shit fits in, I'd love to hear it.

TUROK 2'S WILD FOG-O-RAMA

February 26, 1999 The original Turok: Dinosaur Hunter for the Nintendo 64 was actually kind of shocking, in some ways: we're talking about a strange period in gaming where 3D acceleration wasn't really a thing yet for personal computers, and the fidelity of the first person experience on consoles compared more than favorably with the PC. As a person who games primarily on computers, I looked upon those fully articulated weapons and wept. After that, the series went steadily downhill. Downhill, and into a black cave that good things never come out of.

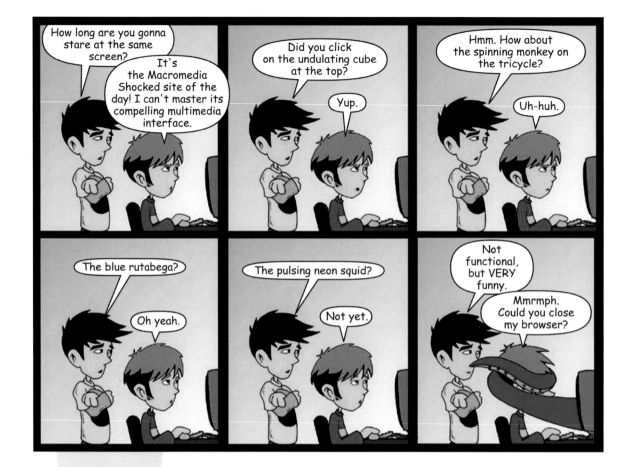

MACROMEDIA FLASHDANCE

March 3, 1999 The level of self-indulgence seen in the first trembling forays of Flash web design was . . . Well, it's comparable to any *Penny Arcade* cartoon ever made.

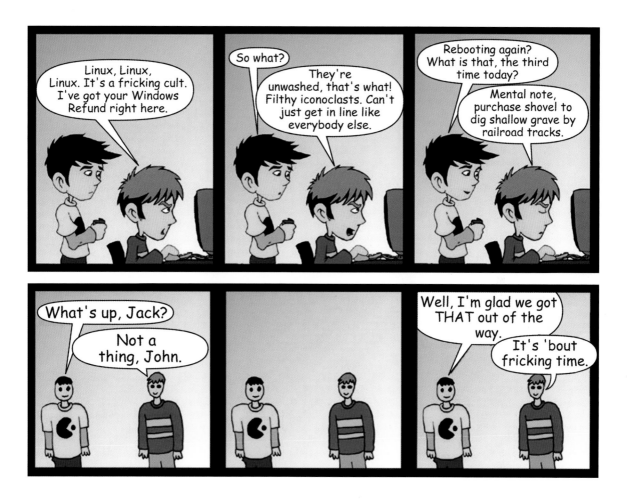

LINUX SHMINUX

March 5, 1999 Linux is an operating system, but it's also a kind of *cult*. There was a movement going to get a rebate on computers purchased with Windows pre-installed. I'm told that those who didn't fall to Microsoft snipers were eventually devoured by "Pitbulls 2.0."

NAMES AT LAST!

March 10, 1999 The first thing you will notice about the next comic is that the art is miserable, be-cause I drew it. The second thing is that they're using names we didn't end up settling on. I don't know if I was trying to be deep or what, but I never had any intention of naming the characters.

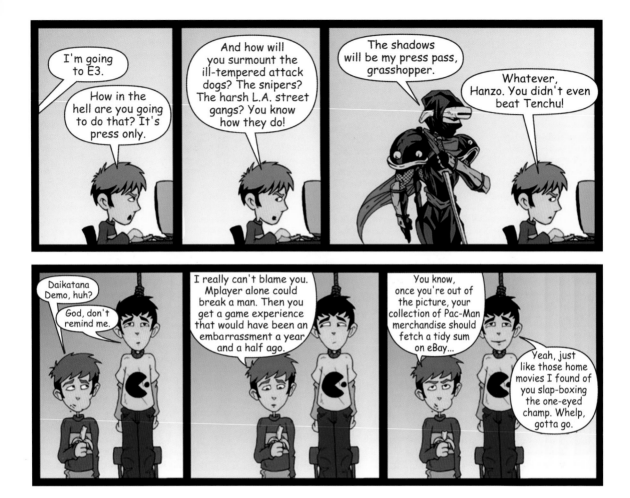

THE ART OF STEALTH AT E3

March 12, 1999 We had to sell our Nintendo 64 to afford it, but we *were* able to attend the Electronic Entertainment Expo. No ninja costumes were required.

DAIKATANA IS DUMB

March 24, 1999 Daikatana would become emblematic of ION Storm, which is unfortunate, especially given their very real successes: games like Anachronox, Deus Ex, and eventually Thief: Deadly Shadows. Pro Tip: Gabriel is referring to my *Penis*.

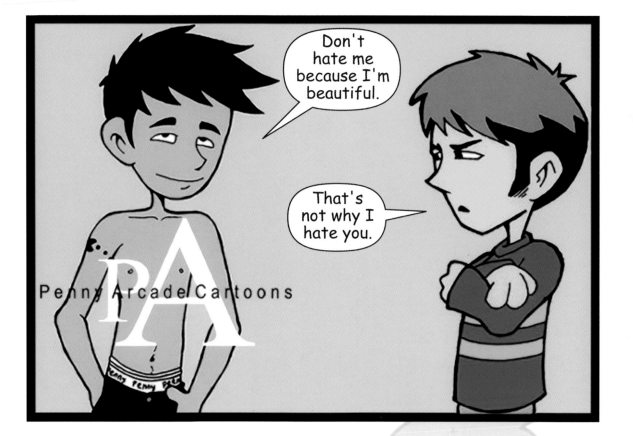

PA ONE—FROM CALVIN KLEIN

March 17, 1999 The Calvin Klein thing, wow. I think we must have been out of town or something and just uploaded some .jpeg lying around on the hard drive.

PA: OGs

March 19, 1999 Still out of town, I think. Are they supposed to be street? You can see the old logo down there, with the scan of a penny, which we must have thought was very clever indeed.

HOT WRESTLING ACTION

March 26, 1999 Wrestling games have always been a kind of guilty pleasure for us. We don't follow the "sport," but we lap up any wrestling title that hits because it's the only genre where hitting a man with a chair is considered even *quasi-legitimate*.

FIRE CAN BE FUN

March 31, 1999 Just look! Look how *desensitized* he is! It is because of the violent video games! Clearly, Tycho has been desensitized to a degree as well, in his skin, because he is on *fire* but is just *standing around*. Kingpin was the GTA: San Andreas of its time, mentioned on the floor of the senate and everything.

A MECH MOMENT FOR US

April 2, 1999 Mechwarrior 3 didn't just *support* 3D acceleration, it gloried in it. My jaw still un-hinges when I think back on it. Seriously, the jaw comes down and my tongue rolls out onto the linoleum, like in *The Mask* starring Jim Carey.

VIDEO GAMES ON TRIAL

April 14, 1999 Even at more than six years old, this comic probably communicates the concept as well as anything we've ever done on the subject. We've gone into more detail on some aspects, but the comic just doesn't need much in the way of introduction.

ILLIAD: NOT FUNNY

April 7, 1999 When we started *Penny Arcade*, there was a comic already running called User Friendly that spoke to a different segment of the geek population. As an April Fool's gag, he suggested that Microsoft had sued him for his satirical assault on Windows. Then, after withdrawing his site from the Intertron, his readers despaired—raising money and being terrified about the assault on free speech. So, we lashed out. I'd like to say that it was because of some *thing* he did, but honestly we'd been chomping at the bit. We were jealous of his success, and it made us behave poorly.

SOFTWARE AND, LIKE, ETC.

April 9, 1999 These days, the people who stock the shelves at a game store usually have a pretty good idea what the fuck is going on. That wasn't always the case.

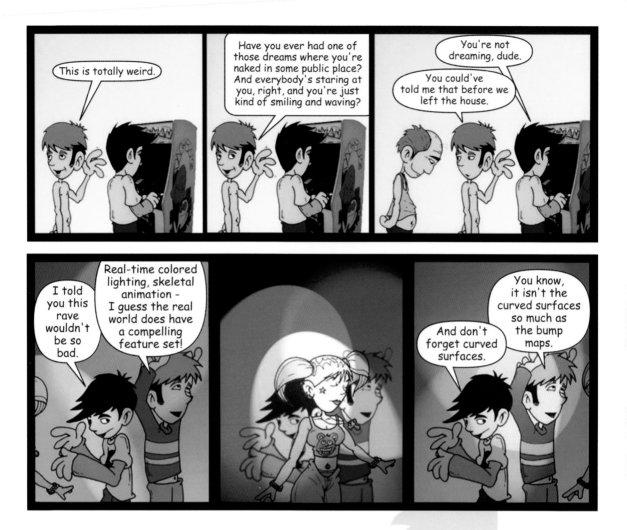

CLOTHING: PROBABLY A GOOD IDEA

April 16, 1999 And then you have *this* one, which is about a naked young man. So you can see that we really do cover all the bases here at *Penny Arcade*.

PA IN DA HOUSE

April 21, 1999 I'm not sure what convinced us to set a comic strip in a Rave, seeing as we've never been to one. I've heard there are girls in attendance who wear candy? Is that true? Because I *do* like candy. I think if they played up the candy angle, attendance would skyrocket.

CHICKA-WOW CHICKA-WOW WOW

April 23, 1999 The milk carton in the fridge is asking if anyone's seen Prey, and oddly enough I *have* seen it. It was already a kind of *urban legend* by the time this comic was made, and it would be another six years before the project resurfaced. I'm *full* of trivia like that.

WHAT BATS?

April 30, 1999 The apartment that birthed this project was revolting to *any* person who did not spend all of their time staring into a monitor. If your nose could have its *own* nightmare, built entirely from olfactory stimuli, it would closely resemble scents we had simply come to expect. A piece of turkey would sometimes lie on the counter for a week, and not because it was asleep or something. We had an evil cat with a urinary tract infection that would deposit a substance like yogurt in places a man could not *physically* clean.

SILLY RABBIT, Q3TEST IS FOR MACS!

April 28, 1999 The rage during this period really was inexpressible for the PC owner, which led us to create vile Macintosh strawman Chuck. Crass, yes, but we were detestable young men. Nothing like the paragons of learning and virtue we have become. It's interesting to remember this time, though, when id still burned like a torch in every gamer's heart. When id began charging for the kind of expansions that Epic gave away for free, goodwill began to deteriorate.

PA: PHILOSOPHY ARCADE?

May 5, 1999 Before I had the news section to expound on this kind of crap, I had to try and coerce Gabe into essentially *drawing* my posts. We have a tenuous creative relationship, one fraught with danger and minefields of ancient disagreements, so horning something like this into a comic just wouldn't be possible anymore. I'd have to take into account a vast matrix of favors and promises made over the course of a decade to even get started. By then, he would literally be asleep.

THREE ATTACKS, ONE STRIP

May 7, 1999 Sometimes you need to dispense a terrific amount of vitriol in a very short amount of time. On this strip, I feel that we approached theoretical limits.

E3: PACMAN D'AMOUR

May 12, 1999 We inadvertently created a tradition the first year we attended E3, the "sketchbook" thing. It sometimes emerges when we're attending other conventions, as well—whenever the full suite of tools aren't available to us. These are the ones from the first year, and they're still some of my favorites.

E3: LET ME DIE!

May 13, 1999

E3: BLIZZARD EMPLOYEE

May 14, 1999

E3: COMPLEX BAGS

May 15, 1999

E3: TYCHO IS DUMB

May 16, 1999

E3: WE ACTUALLY SAW THIS!

May 17, 1999

E3: PACMAN EROTICA II

May 18, 1999

NOTHING TO SEE HERE!

May 25, 1999 People often think they are being extremely clever when they say things like this about our comic, but we sort of already said it five years ago, and we included a handy visual aid. Sooooo . . . Next comic.

INSPIRED BY THE MOVIE

June 9, 1999 Gabriel takes every opportunity to emasculate me when he draws his little *pictures*. I delight in depicting him as a kind of hyperactive rodent, so in the final analysis it's probably a wash.

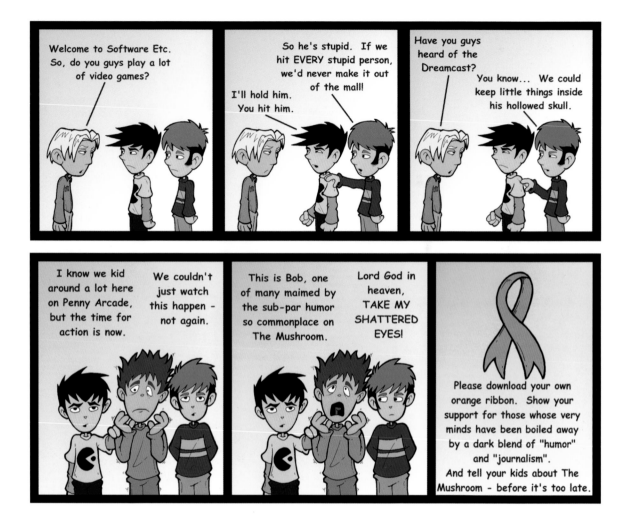

THEY'RE BAAAAAAAACK

June 11, 1999 This is another theme that runs through the comic, apparently—confrontations with software store employees. As I mentioned before, these days we've come to rely on those stalwart crews. They send us pictures of their new summon in Final Fantasy XI, and we go to their birthday parties. Those days, it was all conflict.

THE MUSHROOM

June 13, 1999 This comic was something we must have found on an old hard drive. Did we have a battle with gaming satire site "The Mushroom" in *Penny Arcade's* infancy? We *must* have.

WHO DA MAN?

June 16, 1999 The best part about type-killing in Quake 3 was that players who were typing had a very conspicuous symbol over their heads when they were doing it. They constituted a delicious kind of *low-hanging fruit* that I took special care to savor.

DIVX EQUALS DEAD

June 18, 1999 This one here is the first instance of Div as a character, and not just as a failed consumer product. We'd go on to introduce other robots, robots with . . . *needs*, but that tale is probably best reserved for a later volume.

COLOR GAME BOY OBSESSION

June 23, 1999 We made a book *before* this one, which was written in 2000, much closer to when the original strips were made. Flipping through it, I learned that this was the first comic we hosted under our own URL. We'd always been a part of "loonygames" before, another site, and when the editor there starting telling us how to write our comic, we decided it was time to tell him to go fuck himself.

FUN WITH FISH

June 25, 1999 The fish comic was written before DNS had propagated to the new site, so it was something people probably wouldn't see unless they were hitting the archives.

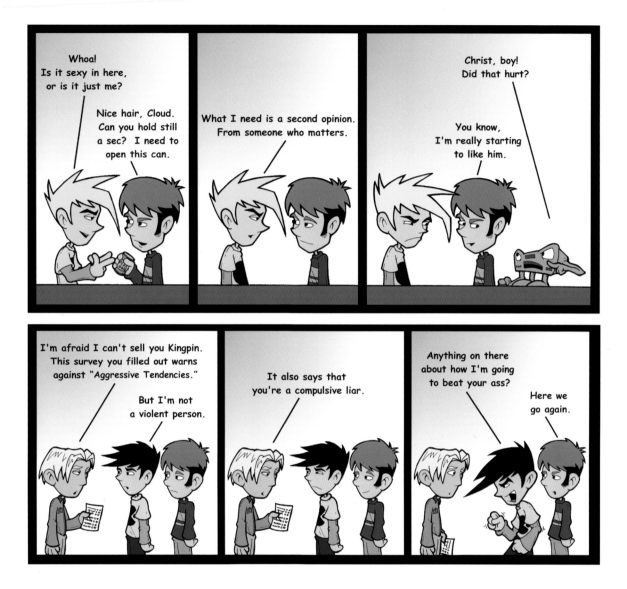

HAIR CITY, POPULATION GABRIEL

June 30, 1999 Kara would actually go on to become a beautician, and Gabriel was sometimes the recipient of these early experiments. It didn't look as bad as I was suggesting, but when you are used to your roommate's head looking a certain way, and then it starts *glowing* or whatever, you take notice.

VIOLENCE SCHMIOLENCE

July 2, 1999 It shames me, but I do believe we spelled "aggressive" incorrectly in this comic. *What will my grammar club say?!?*

GABE'S POCKET MONSTER

July 14, 1999 Gabe goes to the Oregon coast with his family every year around this time, and he usually does watercolors and sketches while he's down there. The one he brought back from this year became a comic. Apparently they spent much of the trip fighting over Pokemon Pinball.

DREAMCAST? OH, YEAH

July 16, 1999 Hollywood Video—are they still a thing?—was renting Dreamcasts before the US launch, and I'll be damned if we weren't the first people in the store. Maybe the only people. As would eventually be shown, the Dreamcast didn't exactly set the world ablaze.

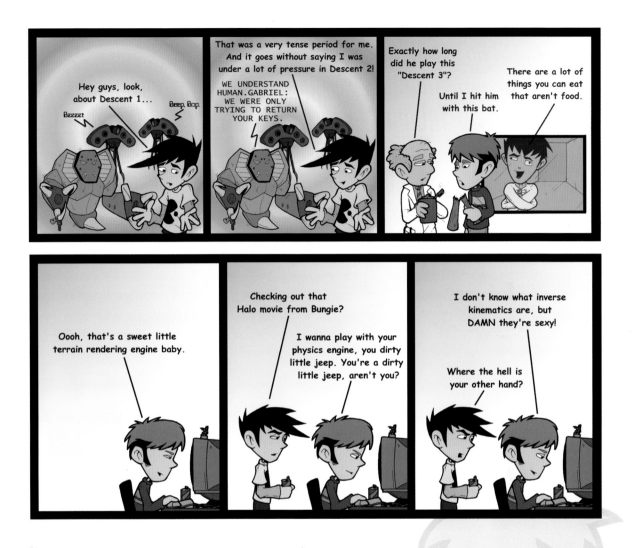

DESCENT INTO MADNESS

July 21, 1999 Descent was a great series that I'd love to see return. Tribes put flight into an FPS and made it *belong*, but by comparison, Descent's hovering craft gave you a sometimes nauseating amount of freedom. The franchise branched out into a series called Descent: Freespace as you'll recall, some of the last great space sims. It's the sort of game one hopes they will meet at the *crossroads*.

HALO: VERY, VERY SEXY

July 23, 1999 Halo would, of course, go on to virtually dominate the world, and you could see some kernel of that experience in the first videos released.

MORTYFIED

July 28, 1999 This comic is probably the only evidence that there ever was a game called Mortyr. We were only doing two comics a week these days, typically in the middle of the night when Gabe got back from work. We got the idea into our heads that comics from a given week would be related in some way, happening in their own continuity. For some reason.

BLEEM ME UP

July 30, 1999 See, because the *computer* is gone!!! Jesus Christ. Bleem, there's another historical artifact. It was actually an emulator for the original Playstation you could run on your PC. You probably knew that. *Nerd.*

SEED OF EVIL

August 4, 1999 We tried this grotesque continuity thing again here, as you'll soon see. Shudder with me. In any case, I have absolutely no recollection of Seed, like everyone else who didn't actively develop it. It used Glide, though—remember *that* shit?

PERCHANCE TO DREAM

August 6, 1999 I think that we planned to utilize this (sigh) "plot point" in the future, and it happened a couple times, but by and large good sense took hold. Oh, the abuse you might have suffered at our hand!

ANOTHER FREE COMIC

August 11, 1999 As the title suggests, I had started to become somewhat *disenchanted* with the instant feedback the Internet offers the creator. Would that I could go back, and offer that younger self succor! I think he would be bolstered by a description of our expansive, private *Penny Arcade* manor-house, with its lions, and peacocks, and . . . You know. *Other* animals.

GONE SHOCKIN'

August 13, 1999 System Shock 2 actually gave me a nervous breakdown. It's possible that other things were going on that I don't recall, but the audio—by Irrational Games' Eric Brosius—gave me nightmares. When I was *awake*.

Z IS FOR ZOMBIE

August 18, 1999 We thought of him as a major player in the strip for a while, and he figures into a couple of my favorite comics from the archive. It's also one of the first comics we did without a gaming theme. At least, I think it is. Flip back a few pages and see.

PVP PLUS PA

August 20, 1999 This was the first comic we'd ever done with another cartoonist online—our erstwhile nemesis, the foul Steve Kuntz from PvP. It was a part of a larger storyline on his site, but it's clear that he shared our enmity for User Friendly. Same reason, I'm guessing.

SOUL (CALIBUR) MATE

August 25, 1999 This grim truth has remained firm, despite strenuous efforts on my part to draw her into the fold. The only exception is The Sims, but that shit's not exactly *hardcore*.

COMMUNICATION

August 27, 1999 God *Damn* we loved us some Soul Reaver. Also, I think this is my favorite comic from the first year of *Penny Arcade*. I'm not saying *you* have to like it or anything, but if you *don't*, I think it kinda says something about you. There, I said it.

SEGA, FULL OF GRACE

September 1, 1999 It's actually Gabe's genuine belief in The Most High that reins me in to the extent that I even *am*. Try to imagine that a believer is responsible for any of this stuff, though. Man, that is some *part-time* spirituality, that's all I'm saying.

H-O-T SPELLS HOT

September 3, 1999 It's clear at this point that we felt John Romero was a kind of humor mine, and we would wheel a cart in there every now and then and emerge with a "joke."

IT'S ABOUT WARCRAFT 3

September 8, 1999 They announced Warcraft 3 with the pomp and fanfare their online announcements are known for, but when you're kinda known for three things, and the other ones already came out, it kinda narrows it down.

HOME SWEET HOMEWORLD

September 19, 1999 One of the other "battles" that characterized early *Penny Arcade* was the one between ourselves and *Daily Radar*, which we had agreed to submit our strips to. Then-editor Aaron Loeb told us that if we wanted to work with *them*, we shouldn't submit crap like *this*. I'm not saying it's the best comic ever, but damn, man: cold! He's gone on to produce *Infected*, which looks like real horseshit.

GABU-SAN

September 15, 1999 Gabriel, who I am told owned *two pair* of the shutter glasses for the Master System, could be always counted on to support Sega—to die in their service, if necessary. There was, however, a small window there where he gamed almost exclusively on the PC. It warmed the heart. The Dreamcast ended all that.

DREAMCASTU!

September 10, 1999 Of course, that's not to say that I didn't *myself* harbor some affection for the device. I'll talk about why a little later in the book, but it was just ahead of its time in a lot of ways.

HOOKERS

September 22, 1999 It seems odd now, but we must have been intimidated by UT's translocators. These kids today, with their *non-standard means of locomotion* and their *hip-hops*, etc.

WORD OF THE DAY: OUTSIDE

September 24, 1999 Affection for this comic strip has remained high. I always liked it.

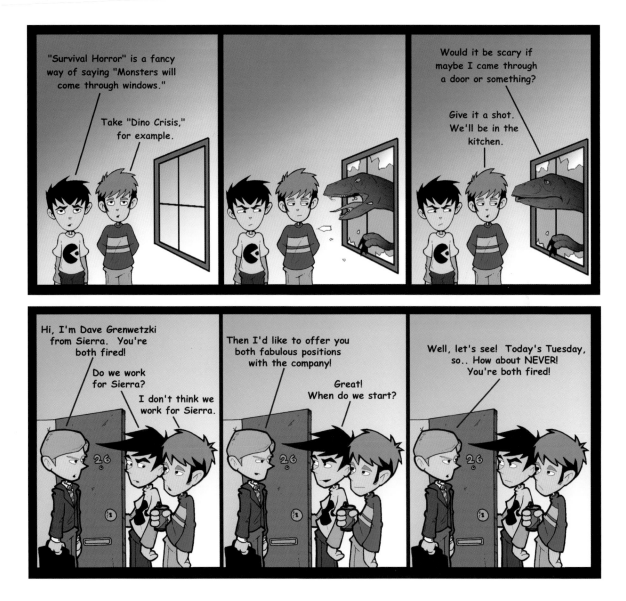

DINO CRISIS SUCKS

September 29, 1999 Dino Crisis, that's not something that anybody liked. A least, I never met anybody who did. I'm not even sure Capcom liked it. An amalgam of Jurassic Park and Resident Evil, it never felt like it did much well.

CHAINSAW DAVE

October 1, 1999 There are a few comics in the archive done to comfort those abused by the industry in general. I'm not sure if we think of it as penance for the abuse we dole out under ordinary circumstances, but the fact of the matter is that these people have provided us with a *hundred hours* of enjoyment and escape. Uploading an image to the web is really the least we can do.

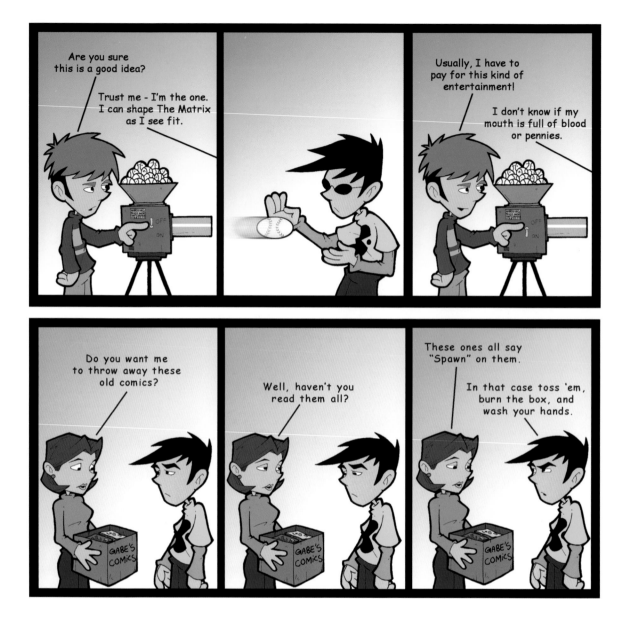

BALLS, COME GET YOUR BALLS

October 6, 1999 This comic is an almost exact duplicate of a comic by that nefarious lie factory, Scott Kurtz. We felt really bad, still do actually, but our feud with him suppresses those genuine sentiments.

IN THAT CASE

October 8, 1999 I would go along with him on these jabs at Todd McFarlane, but as a young man I spent my time dialed into this or that BBS, and the world of comics was unknown to me. It was Gabriel's rage at Todd that would culminate in Dr. Raven Darktalon Blood.

GABRIEL: 1977-1999

October 13, 1999 It wasn't Gabe, it was me, and it was Monster Rancher as opposed to Battle Arena Toshinden. I never *did* bring it back. When I was trying to get a house, it came up on my credit report. I think that basically makes me King of the Monster Ranchers.

GET DOWN TONITE X2

October 15, 1999 Gabriel and I certainly *had* bachelor parties, but they were defined more by Soul Calibur 2 than debauchery. It was purely business as usual. As I said in the first book, the only thing that distinguished these supposed "bachelor" parties from any other day was that everyone treats you like you're about to die.

BOOB RAIDER

October 18, 1999 Up to this point, we'd always just written the comics together in the apartment while we played games and hung out, a "style" that was "cramped" by my impending marriage. I don't regret it or anything, but, I mean, God damn. That was a hell of a setup.

TERMINAL REALITY

October 20, 1999 No. Fucking. Idea.

DON'T SAY IT!

October 22, 1999 It doesn't happen a lot, but if you end up with some kind of Zombie Problem at your public pool, I can't stress this enough: do not engage in the customary games! This is what Zombies *expect*.

THIS WON'T HURT A BIT

October 24, 1999 Gabe used to have one of those zipper cases full of games, all systems, it was like a leather museum detailing the history of the medium. I'd just hand that shit out to anybody that came over. Tomb Raider was the least of it.

HE'S JUST THIRSTY

October 27, 1999 Here's another drunken robot! So we clearly have some kind of thing going. It was a play off the "Sega Dreamcast: It's Thinking" campaign, but there's no reason anyone should know that anymore. I'm glad I'm typing these.

FEELING HOT, HOT, HOT

October 29, 1999 The urge to work an upcoming holiday into a comic, sitcom-style, can be intense. The results haven't been universally delicious. That said, we *have* done some cool holiday shits: The Last Christmas and The Fall of the House of Brahe come to mind.

WATCH OUT

November 1, 1999 This is where "The Watch" thing started, apparently. From such tiny seeds! His collection of Pac-Man artifacts hasn't gotten any smaller. From where I'm sitting right now, I can see no less than *twelve*.

RAWHIDE

November 3, 1999 You can't even do a joke about Duke Nukem Forever anymore. It's not possible. The ridicule it has amassed by this point is so dense that it forms a kind of armor that satire can't penetrate.

I'LL CRY IF I WANT TO

November 5, 1999 Ho, ho! *Sheesh.*

HE LOVES ME NOT

November 8, 1999 You can't really pretend to be surprised when we depict an act of *intense violence* in our comics anymore. Not only has a lifetime of playing evil video games warped our sense of right and wrong, transforming us into little more than animals, it's one of the things that define *Penny Arcade*. I'm not sure what people thought these mails would accomplish.

(INSERT WIND SOUND HERE)

November 10, 1999 More lashing out, this time toward Penny Arcade's crucible, the online 'zine loonygames. His site had come back briefly after we left, but the content on offer was pretty slim. I'm not sure what convoluted lesson he was supposed to learn from this comic.

WELCOME TO PAIN CITY

November 12, 1999 Soldier of Fortune as a series has the most repulsive hit models of any games ever released for any system, but they're never brought up as examples because the people who decry video games as entertainment don't have any fucking clue what they're talking about.

CUP O' SUNSHINE

November 15, 1999 Gabriel brought this "sideways, up your ass" thing back from work one day, and we thought it was a fantastic, you know, *technique* or whatever. It ended up in a strip without us knowing that it was a catchphrase from The World Wrestling Federation. We did not watch R.A.W., you understand. We were not R.A.W. watchers.

THE BOSS OF YOU

November 17, 1999 Um, Age of Empires guys? Ensemble Studios? Is it okay if we use this screen-shot? When we started making *Penny Arcade*, we didn't think anyone would like it enough to *want* a book.

WITH SPECIAL GUEST

November 19, 1999 The way we represent Him is considered sacrilegious by some readers, but Gabe reels me in considerably on Jesus as a "character." And, since he draws it, it's not like I can just *slip it in*. He's not going to get done drawing it, and be like "Oh, he's throwing up the horns, *from the cross*."

FUNNY ALL BY ITSELF

November 22, 1999 Then, as today, "Daikatana" equals instant merriment! The word itself is over ninety percent joy. The rest, as I understand it, is carob.

I THINK IT'S WORKING

November 24, 1999 I don't know if there's supposed to be a port on there, or on *me*, or what. At any rate, this is the sort of thing you could really hurt yourself doing. Unless your penis is USB 2.0, I wouldn't even attempt it.

GABRIEL GAIDEN

November 29, 1999 One: it's probably not the tooth fairy. Two: that is clearly some kind of God-damn ninja! So, I'm guessing you can wish all night without making a real dent in the Ninja Issue.

FROM ANOTHER DIMENSION

December 1, 1999 Ultima IX actually had some truly amazing *game* in there, for all the technical issues. It wasn't really their fault, I don't think. Origin was trying to finish an extremely ambitious project during a time of intense turbulence in consumer 3D. It's a shame.

(IN)SECURITY

December 3, 1999 The Quake 3 test—and I hope I am remembering this correctly—returned to id some data about your hardware configuration. Quake 3 test, you understand. The *test version*, they were using to determine their performance on different hardware. I never saw the problem. Most people were just happy to finally play it.

THERE'S NO GOOD REASON

December 8, 1999 It's said that the Rage Wars were the most intense wars of all, because, um . . . Yeah, I've got nothing.

I WANNA SEE S.T.A.R.S

December 10, 1999 So, Dino Wars or Dino Crisis or whatever never did it for us, not even the one that took place in space, where you fought a dinosaur on an orbital station. When you write it out like that, it sounds so *good*. We loved Resident Evil, though. And honestly, if the series just had to survive long enough to make it to Resident Evil 4, it *still* would have been worth it.

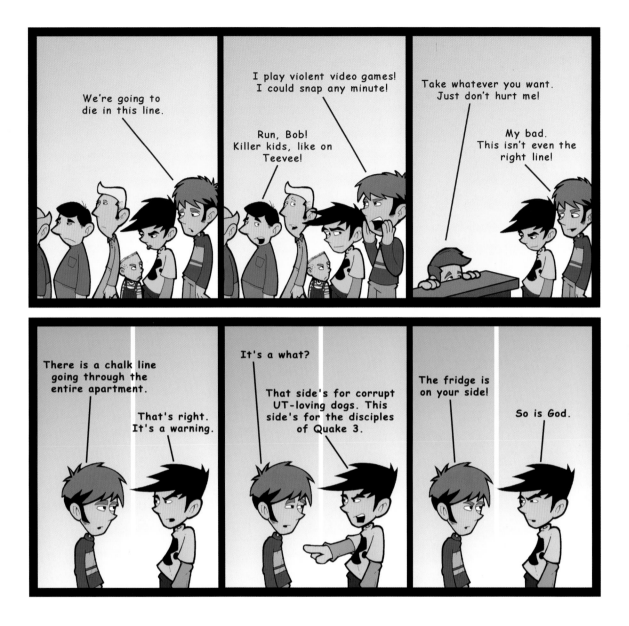

THE LONGEST LINE

December 13, 1999 This still works, actually. You might need to mention a game from Rockstar specifically, just to give it that extra punch—throw something in there they'll recognize from CNN. If possible, try to have a graph of some kind with you. Nod gravely as you display it.

INFIDELS

December 15, 1999 So, this was a big deal at the time, this battle of the pure shooters, two heavy-hitters fighting over the total playerbase. These days, there's no question that user-created *mods* dominate the raw numbers. The way that a popular game *itself* becomes a platform has really been something to see.

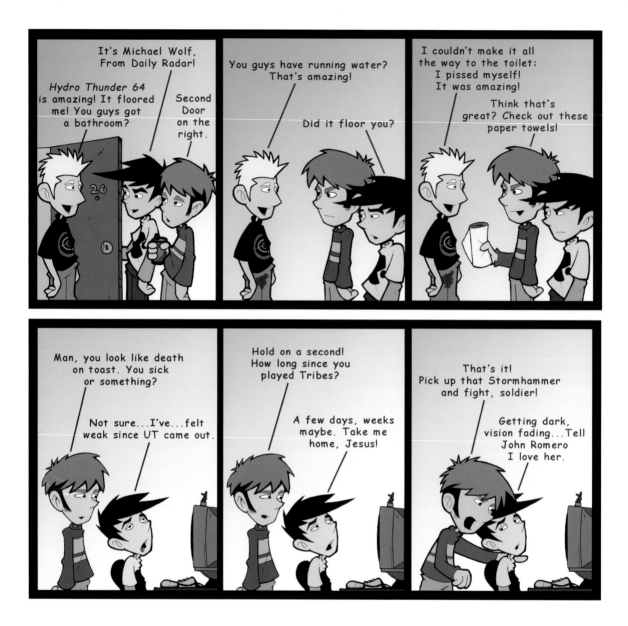

VIVA LA MOISTURE

December 17, 1999 We've met Michael Wolf a couple times, actually, since this comic went up – he's really very nice. He mailed us back when it was "published," saying that he looked nothing like his representation, and I told him he'll look any way I want him to Goddamn look. Such is the dark power of the comic author.

I'VE SEEN THESE SYMPTOMS

December 19, 1999 You've got just a *touch* of Romero in there, tastefully executed. But it really is surprising how long we played the original Tribes. No game since has exerted that kind of control, short of World of Warcraft anyway, which is really more of a lifestyle.

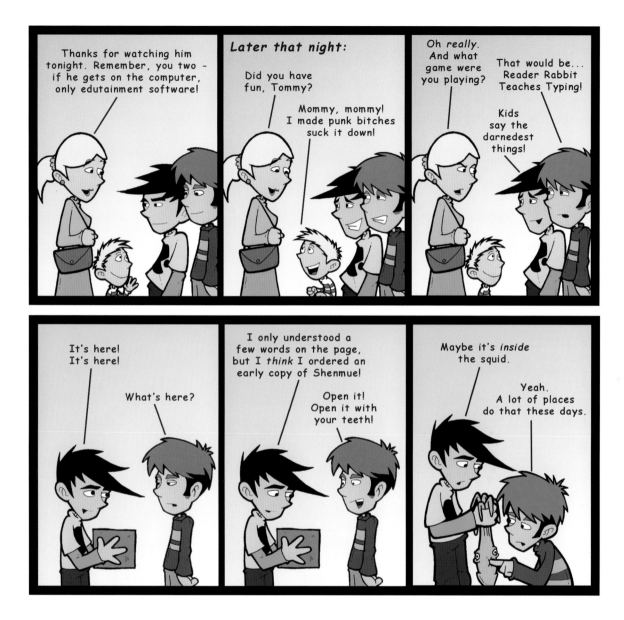

A THREAT TO AMERICA'S YOUTH

December 20, 1999 No person in their right mind would make us even *temporary* stewards of their children, this much is certain. As Gabriel is now aware, there is a *loophole* in place when you create the child yourself.

GUARANTEED FRESH

December 22, 1999 Even before the release of Shenmue, Yu Suzuki's oddly compelling paean to nineteen-eighties Japan already had a kind of grip on me. I knew importing a game that language-dense was a crazy proposition, so I resisted the impulse. Importing stuff these days is fairly straightforward. Then, as you can see, we were intimidated by the range of potential failures.

I'VE GOT YOUR JOLLY RIGHT HERE

December 24, 1999 My favorite part about this comic is Santa's grasping little claw in the second panel, a finger configuration that just screams, "I don't mind if I *do.*" Why Tycho would have a plunger in the last panel isn't clear to me now, and I'm terrified to think what purpose it might serve.

PA TOURNAMENT EDITION

December 26, 1999 In an alternate dimension, perhaps there is a version of this comic worth commenting on. Do you remember when I said that I might need to be held? *Hold me.*

HAIL TO THE KING

December 27, 1999 I don't know if there is a gamer these days that garners the kind of attention Thresh did at the time. There's a considerably more sophisticated pro-gamer infrastructure in place, but . . . Wait, is that a tiny Boba Fett on the monitor? Has that been there the whole time?

THE BOY AIN'T RIGHT

December 29, 1999 With the sorts of things people are worrying about today, the Y2K thing is almost ethereal by comparison. I'd love to go back to worrying about a couple stray numbers in the middle of the night instead of our current apocalypse.

PA2K

December 30, 1999 I mean, it's really what some people thought was going to happen. We'd invented machines to keep track of things for us, but we'd done it in the myopic way we do every other Goddamn stupid thing, and since we all believe *deep down* that there's a man coming to settle accounts, we were primed for the end of all things.

Were rocks going to turn to liquid? Was the boiling point of water at sea level going to change? Here's a man on the news, come to scare you half to death. Here's a preacher man talking about how it goes down at the end of *his* book. It's like people expected His Terrible Swift Sword to pierce the Earth, and the two halves would split wet like a melon, and we'd fly into fucking space.

THE DIFFERENCE

January 3, 2000 If I've been good, sometimes I can coax some of this cybervixen activity to the fore. These days, obviously a mere *gig* is insufficient. These days it's more about terabytes and RAID and data striping. You know what I'm saying? *Rowrr.*

PSSSST . . . GOD HATES GABE

January 5, 2000 Gabe was invited to Gamespy's News Year's party back in 2000, which I guess we can assume was called "Beatdown." The rest of the story played out as you see here.

MONKIFICATION COMPLETE

January 7, 2000 Blue is the proprietor of Blue's News, still going strong, and in Penny Arcade's ancient past he and the guy from loonygames were trying to get us into some kind of affiliate thing. Nothing ever came of it, which is usually how that kind of thing goes. At the time, we must have seen this as some kind of attack on him. I can't possibly imagine how.

ITSY, BITSY, FUZZY, WUZZY

January 10, 2000 If you could read *my* mind right now, it would say "Let's move on to the next comic."

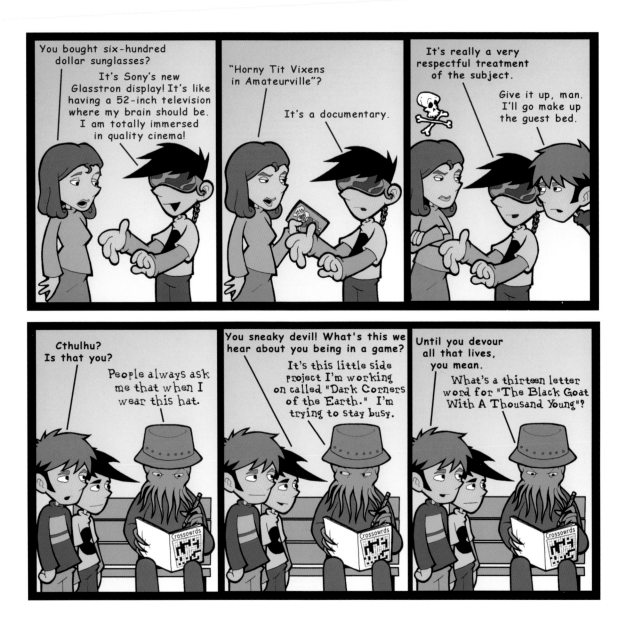

WHILE YOU'RE AHEAD

January 12, 2000 He really did get a pair of these things, but I'm not aware that he took advantage of any specific *genre*, if you get my meaning. I'd come over to write the strip sometimes, and he'd just be spread out on the floor, Glasstron on his head, his mouth forming silent words.

INCOGNITO

January 14, 2000 Now *this* is hard to believe—but Dark Corners of the Earth, announced back in 2000, is finally coming out in *2006*. Given the span of time we're talking about, there can be no doubt that this project is animated by some unseemly, potentially malevolent force.

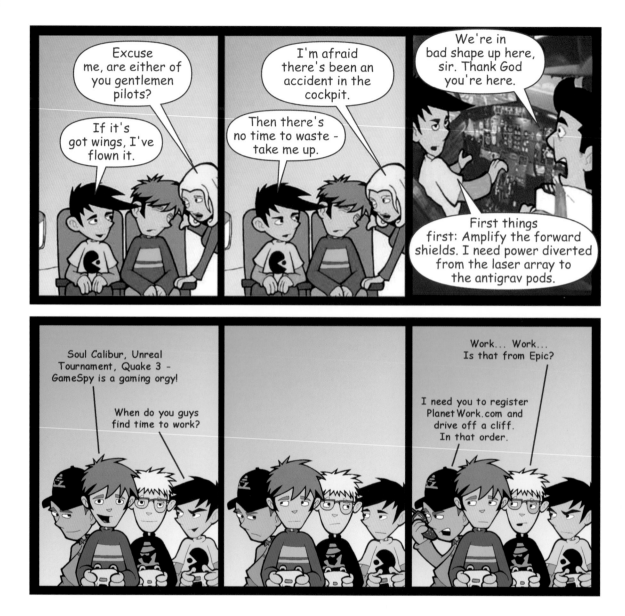

GOT SKILLZ?

January 19, 2000 It's fun to imagine that I've accrued some genuine knowledge in my quest to achieve more potent "skillz" in the digital realm. There may be scenarios in which I could represent our species well. If alien invasions occurred with greater frequency, I think I could really distinguish myself.

MMMM . . . SMELLS LIKE SOULS

January 21, 2000 Gamespy invited us down to their office densely packed with gamers to, I *think*, try to hire us. It was some amazing fantasy come to life. Gabe eventually took them up on it. You can still see his art all over their site. I chose instead to meditate on a rocky crag while I perfected my martial arts.

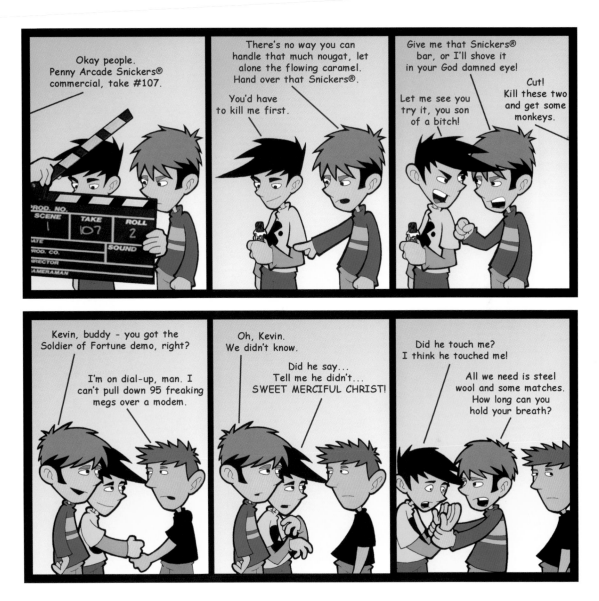

PA SELL-OUTS

January 24, 2000 I have always heard the cries of "sell-out" from atop my mountain fortress. Everyone always believes they are more virtuous than every other person. These people often feel as though *they* haven't sold out, when the reality is that they have nothing worth buying. I submit to you that these are two different things.

LIKE LEPERS, BUT . . . WORSE

January 26, 2000 We were one of the first hundred "households" in Spokane, Washington to get broadband as part of a USWest pilot program. It *immediately* segregated the gaming population, creating a kind of crystalline tower ensconced by a data ghetto. I built a computer for my mom a couple weeks ago, and installing a modem in an otherwise top-of-the-line machine was the hardest thing I've ever had to do.

MOVE OVER, HELL

January 28, 2000 Touch-tone menu systems are *expressly designed* to obstruct genuine assistance; it's really sort of the point. It isn't hard to believe that there is a scheming, disembodied intellect responsible for your pain. In fact, it's superior to the alternative, which is that another human being designed it, made it like a *cage* to catch you.

CLICK HERE TO SEND HATE-MAIL

January 31, 2000 Slashdot is a fixed coordinate in the geek universe, as stable as anything there is—as I was typing this, even the *spell checker* knew to capitalize it. Maybe the computer itself reads it while I'm in the bathroom. It is, however, possible to overdose on raw Linux orthodoxy, entering a kind of "nerd trance" state.

AN EXTRA HELPING

February 2, 2000 Gaming luminary Graeme Devine said gamers were often introverted and socially inept, and then we responded in *this* way, and it has taken me years to realize that he'd basically predicted how we would respond. Well played, Mr. Devine. *Well played.*

THE RAIN

February 4, 2000 This is my favorite Zombie comic, obviously, because, I mean, look at him out there in the rain. While I've got you here, Zombie Revenge is one of the best games Sega ever made. I think we're the minority opinion on that, but if there is another game that will let you grind a zombie to nothing with a gigantic industrial drill, *I've* certainly never heard of it.

CONDIMENTS

February 9, 2000 We'd have an opportunity to bring back the Answertron almost immediately, when my potent Voodoo 2 got boned somehow. Boned is an engineering term. Engineers be using that shit nonstop.

AROUND THE WORLD: 15 MINUTES

February 7, 2000 We sometimes break with geek orthodoxy on some issues. We like our free shit as much as the next person, maybe *more*, but it's hard to take a man seriously when they say that Napster's primary purpose was not to shuttle copyrighted music from computer to computer for free.

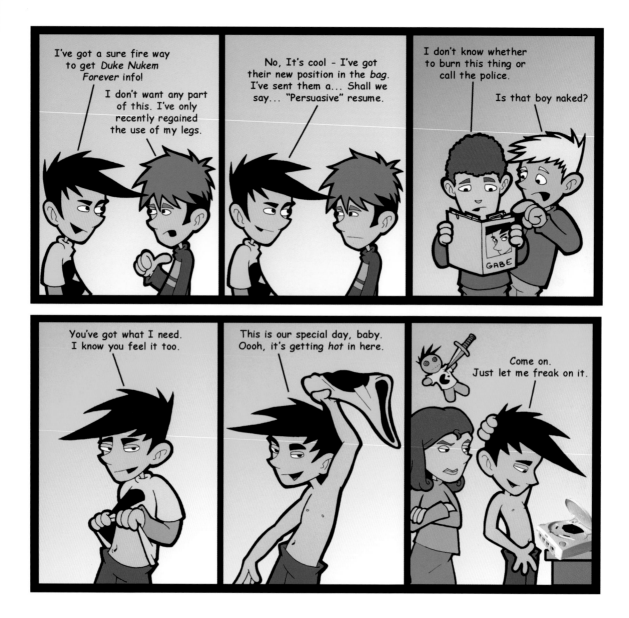

JOB, IN THE CLASSIC SENSE

February 11, 2000 This comic was written when it was widely believed that Duke Nukem Forever *was* still being made, it was just being made at a glacial rate by a single narcoleptic lemur.

HE DOES THIS A LOT

February 14, 2000 We made jokes about it or whatever, but he loved that fucking thing. He never *literally* loved it, not to the best of my knowledge, but he did have one that stopped working under mysterious circumstances. Might be best if we didn't go tugging on that particular thread.

SABABABABWA

February 16, 2000 One of the reasons he loved the Dreamcast so much is that Sega went hog wild on it, cracking out inventive instant classics like Chu Chu Rocket. Four people could play it together, online, thousands of mice running headlong into a cat's *mouth*, what was known as a "Mouse Apocalypse."

HE'S SO DREAMY

February 18, 2000 I think he probably didn't deserve all this shit from us. He made Doom, and it's a fact that his long, lustrous hair just makes a man feel safe. I just want to get wrapped up in there and forget about the cares of the world.

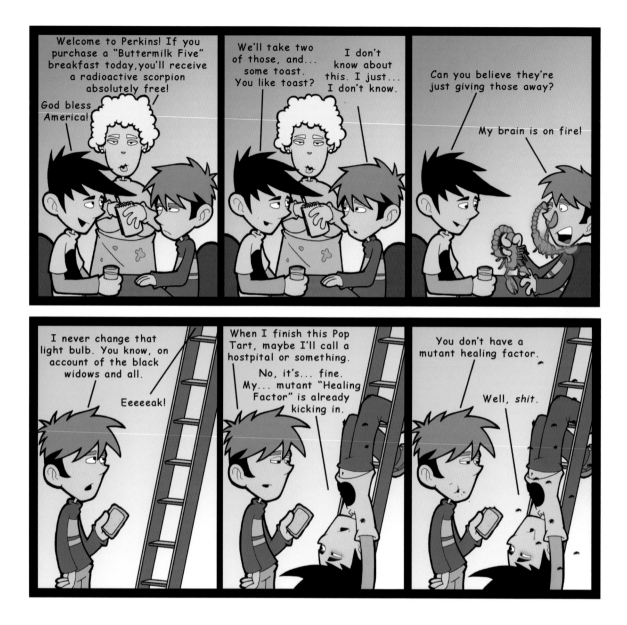

I'VE GOT SOMETHING IN MY EYE

February 21, 2000 We'd write strips at Perkins, basically a Denny's or a Shari's plus a bakery. The day we wrote this, they had some batshit offer where you could buy like forty fucking muffins, and then they would give you a few more, which was the last Goddamn thing you needed right about then.

ALONG CAME A SPIDER

February 23, 2000 This was Gabriel's favorite strip for going on five years. I can't imagine why, as it clearly depicts his avatar's broken body covered in a black rug of poisonous spiders. There is a Pop Tart in there, I guess. Maybe he thinks those are really good.

OBSCURE QUOTE GOES HERE

February 25, 2000 Crazy Taxi was not a game we progressed very far in.

PA: THE REDEMPTION

February 28, 2000 Sometime before the dawn of civilization, Nihilistic—who would go on to develop much of Starcraft: Ghost—made a game based on White Wolf's *Vampire: The Masquerade*. We got carried away with the more "stake-oriented" elements of the mythos and neglected to mention the game itself.

THANKS FOR CLEARING THAT UP

March 1, 2000 This was always a strip the stalwart *Penny Arcade* reader could point to and say, "See? See?" to people who didn't take games *or* the site seriously.

THE ASS FILES

March 3, 2000 I can recall being so invigorated as I sat down to watch that week's *X-Files*, the one written by William Gibson, the patron saint of *dorks*. It might have been the worst episode ever made, and they had a show with a monster who eats *tumors*.

THE RIGHT TO REMAIN JUICY

March 6, 2000 Arby's is really the thread that runs through our work, binding it together. Without that delicious . . . "meat," our work would not be possible.

OVERNIGHT DELIVERY . . . OF DOOM

March 8, 2000 We'll play any old survival horror game, even *Carrier*, referenced here. We're suckers for the genre, but Dreamcast owners couldn't really afford to be picky game-wise. Our patience would eventually be rewarded with Resident Evil: Code Veronica, riches beyond our wildest imaginings. I *think* imaginings is a word.

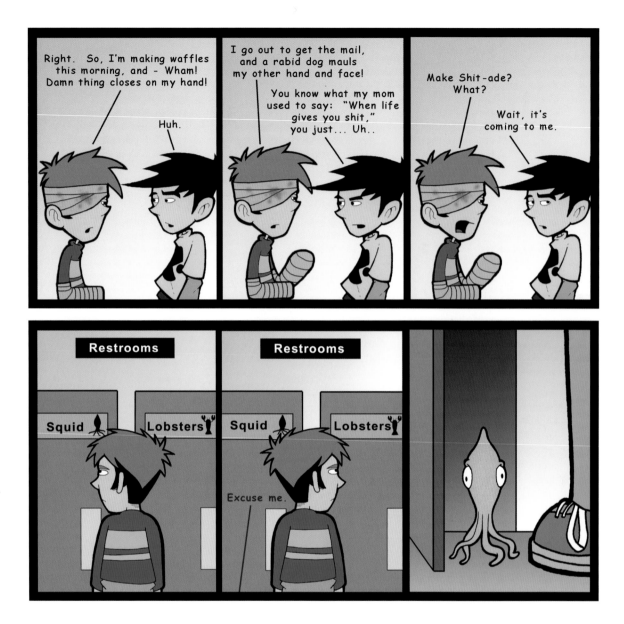

PAIN DOT COM

March 10, 2000 He can draw a purty picture, but do not count on the man to *soothe the soul*. Certainly not without intense physical discomfort on his part.

TWO PATHS DIVERGED

March 13, 2000 Bathrooms have always been places of terror and confusion for me, and when restaurants feel the need to specify the genders in *foreign languages* or with *science fiction races* it really compounds the fear.

MONKEY BIDNESS

March 15, 2000 I'm waiting for someone to punch a monkey at the zoo or something, and blame flash ads. You *know* that shit is coming.

NOW, PICTURE IT VICIOUS

March 17, 2000 For a while, we always had Kara's dialogue be a symbol of some kind. You can see it in a couple other strips. We're not trying to reinforce negative gender stereotypes with Kara and Brenna, I have to emphasize that: they are simply much smarter, much braver, more pragmatic people.

DIABLO II: BUT AT WHAT PRICE?

March 20, 2000 Even after one application of Lucky Rat™, I start to see real change in my life!!! So strong with Rat!!!! I kill man in single combats!!! THANK YOU, LUCKY RAT™!!!

UP ON THE ROOFTOP

March 22, 2000 Dead or Alive had a feature where—and this is serious—the older you said you were, the more "bounce" the female characters had. This is a real thing, and I'm not making it up. We turned it all the way up, and I don't know if a ninety-nine-year-old man is ready for that.

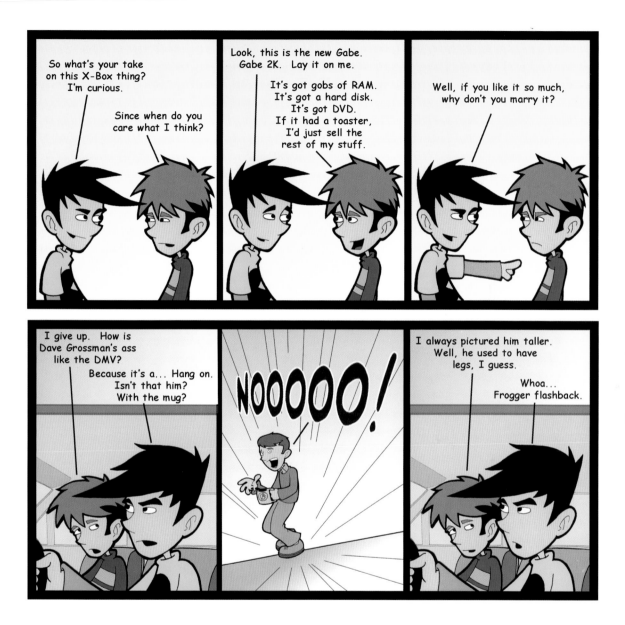

I KNOW YOU ARE

March 24, 2000 It would take a while for the Xbox to really prove itself to us. Something you might not have heard: in Japan, there was a reality show where a family of seven actually lived *inside* one for a month. It was called *Darkness Place Goujanshi.*

HOW MANY POINTS IS THAT?

March 27, 2000 Before Jack Thompson there was *Dave Grossman*, the man who brought us the word "Killology." Before them it was Tipper Gore, back when they thought society's big problem was unregulated rap *music*.

BY MOVIE, YOU MEAN CRAP

March 29, 2000 Man, you can't *run* a scam like this on the girl. She went to college! She knows all about your shit!

MORE MONSTERS MEANS MORE FUN

March 31, 2000 One of those sets of eyes is actually Brenna's, who (in a feat I've never been able to repeat) actually played the entire game with us. For a week, we'd get together in the evenings and be scared to death. It was *delicious*.

HEAT IN A CAN

April 5, 2000 If I was there with you, I'd just put my forearm over this strip and direct you to the next comic. I'd really be doing you a favor.

RIGHT. UH-HUH. SURE

April 7, 2000 If you ever see this game poking out of a bargain bin or something, don't hesitate. I'm sure it's already in that weird section, you know the one I'm talking about—it'll be at, like, *Best Buy,* and it's got a lot of clip art and foreign language crap. Just dig around.

IT'S ACTUALLY A GIRL

April 10, 2000 Of course, it *was* coming, and it was *excellent*—but how could we know? It's a lesson our young hero would learn hard.

THE METROID SAGA, PART 2

April 12, 2000 I am honestly freaking out! How will it end?!?!? I can't imagine that they'd just write it as they went along without any plan whatsoever!

THE METROID SAGA, PART 3

April 14, 2000 A three-part storyline? That is some epic shit—and it's an example of both Gabe's exquisite art and my own prodigious narrative gifts. There are a lot of subtleties there, shot through the panels like veins of some precious metal.

$50: ALL NIGHT TECH SUPPORT

April 17, 2000 As I mentioned before, we never really needed an excuse to lash out at User Friendly's author, Illiad—but we had at least a glimmer of purpose, this time. He was trying to launch the strip as a media company, and the site detailed what demographic each of his characters could best manipulate. It was odd.

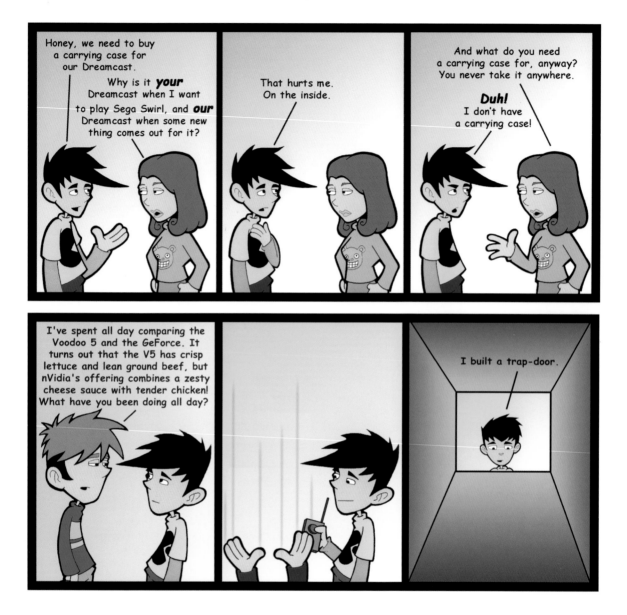

GABE 0, KARA 1

April 19, 2000 The desire for a console carrying case is so primal in its power that I don't even know how I would argue for it. I've tried to simulate it in my mind, and it largely amounts to a series of unintelligible, earnest gestures.

IDLE HANDS

April 21, 2000 I guess there's something going on here, beef, and trap doors I guess, but it's just hard to imagine that there's really no such thing as 3dfx anymore. You'd buy a game, and it didn't have generic 3D support—it had 3dfx *specific* support. If you played PC games, you essentially had to own one.

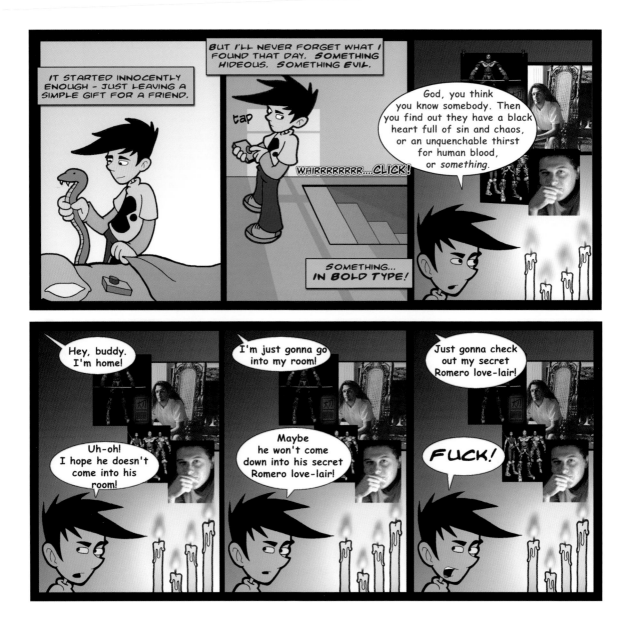

SHOCKING REVELATION

April 24, 2000 No longer content to merely name check, we wove John Romero into a powerful tale—our *magnum opus*. I need to look that word up and make sure it means what I think it does. It's either a creative work or a rich sauce.

TENSION . . . BUILDING

April 26, 2000 The reality is that I think we had begun to feel a little guilty about having mistreated him. The idea that one of us secretly deified the man seemed like a kind of honor we could pay him.

THRILLING CONCLUSION

April 28, 2000 Aaaaand . . . There you have it. Have you been changed irrevocably? Let's just pause here for a moment and think about all the irrevocable changes.

TONIGHT, ON TOO DAMN LATE

May 1, 2000 A couple things: one, we worship Bruce Campbell, and the chance to pee on him— even in a piece of fiction—really was an honor. Two, he lent a lot of character to Tachyon. I'm trying to remember if I really enjoyed the game, or if I really enjoyed *space sims*, and was just happy somebody made one.

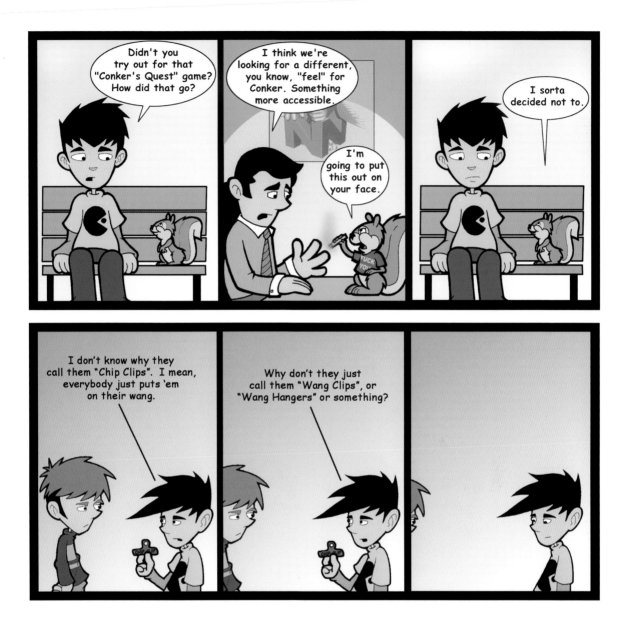

BENCH ARCADE

May 2, 2000 I *guess* this is a crossover, but it's with our sister site The Bench, and I don't know if you can actually "crossover" with yourself without grievous injury. Also, this was before Conker got all R rated, so the comic makes *no sense*.

GOD HELP US

May 5, 2000 People still bring us chip clips at conventions from time to time, which is kind of cool, but also . . . Hmm. You know? *Hmm.*

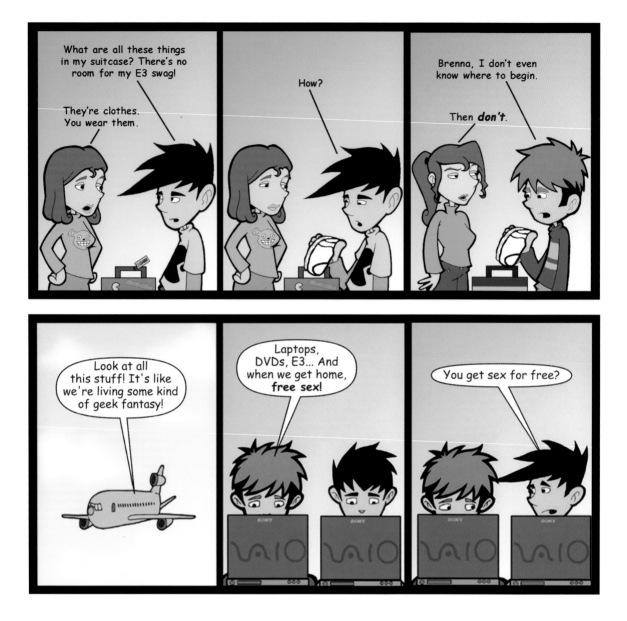

SURE, IT'S COTTON ... BUT WHAT IS IT?

May 8, 2000 We actually have a super elaborate system for E3 packing, refined over the course of several years. It involves placing luggage *inside* of other luggage. We totally invented that, so if you use it, you have to give me five dollars.

THIS COMIC GOT ME IN TROUBLE

May 10, 2000 It really was the height of insanity. Just before E3, we'd signed a contract with a "content aggregator," a Dot Com Boom invention that promised to pay us to do *Penny Arcade*. It seemed like a pretty awesome deal at the time. It wasn't.

E32K: THE HAT CONUNDRUM

May 11, 2000 We would maintain the tradition in the second year, and the wonders we saw will *astound* you. Feast your eyes upon them, and be amazed!

E32K: THE EYES HAVE IT

May 12, 2000

E32K: SOMEONE SHOOT HIM

May 13, 2000

BIOWARE'S BOUNTY

May 17, 2000 We were unprepared to deal with the huge tub of beer and glass platters stacked high with sandwiches, but our new friends from the north insisted that we take full advantage. Even then, I think they might have been shocked when I turned the full force of my dark appetite on their supply.

IT'S IN THE STANDS!

May 19, 2000 I don't know what would have possessed us to do this comic. We don't know anything about sports, I have only a passing familiarity with the people who play them professionally, and the whole thing is unconnected to Warcraft. Love the glowing sigils on the bat, though.

111

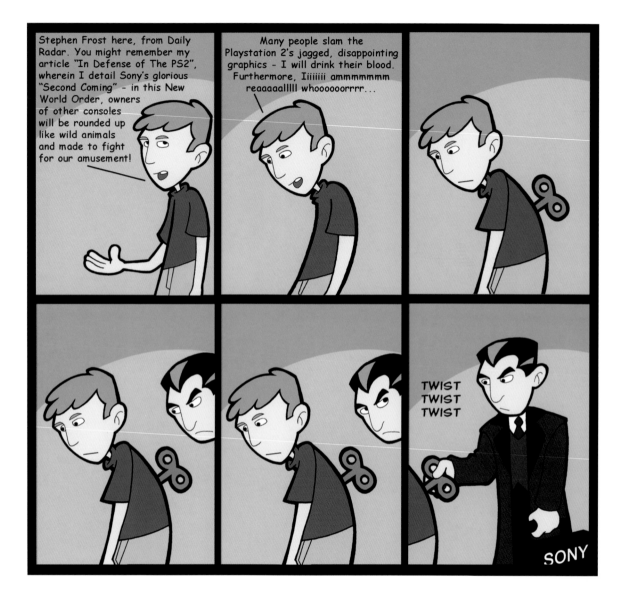

LET'S DO THE TWIST

May 22, 2000 This comic can be seen as a skirmish in the larger war with *Daily Radar*, our defeated foe—but it was hard to believe that we'd been to the same show and seen the same things he had. This is basically a political cartoon; it's just about something the culture at large doesn't care about.

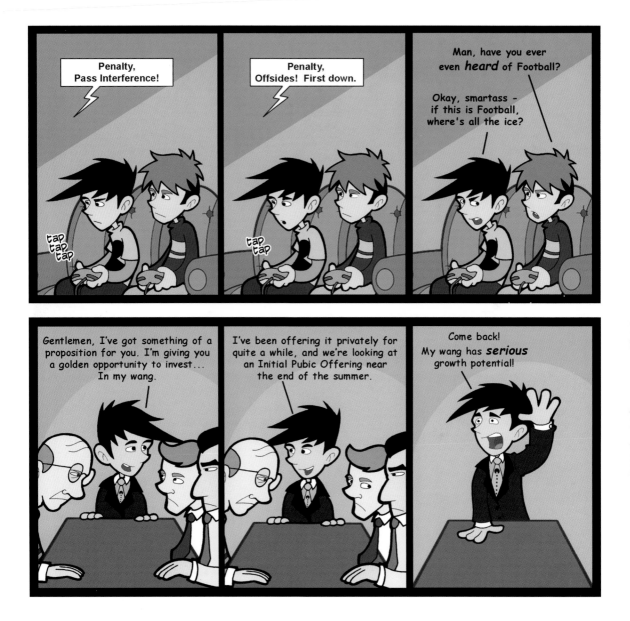

SEE THAT GUY? HIT HIM

May 24, 2000 It turns out that we really *like* sports games, when we remember to buy them. We played NFL2K1 online quite a bit, which was unlike anything we'd ever done. Three people would play the actual game while Gabe would talk trash with a keyboard plugged into port 4. Marvelous.

THIS COULD BE BIG

May 26, 2000 We don't actually use the word that often, a handful of times over the course of seven years, but it has doggedly remained some kind of *emblem*.

LOOKING GLASS 4 EVER

May 29, 2000 Many of their human beings, animated by the inventive spirit that characterized the company, continue to produce amazing things over at Irrational Games. The world is a better place for it.

WHEN MONKEYS ATTACK

May 31, 2000 I'm told that the concept artist was actually very angry about this comic, but given his frenetic, terrifying work it was clear that the man operated from a *core* of pure rage.

K-MART SAVING LIVES

June 2, 2000 It's more complicated than this—but I've never been able to understand how, in all the talk about violent media, the specific *tools* that allow these rampages never come up. It would be like if there was a rash of *gardening* nationwide, but nobody mentioned spades or hoes.

BETTY, FETCH MY PITCHFORK

June 5, 2000 Here's one of those "comfort cartoons" I mentioned. Kelly Flock sent me a mail after this comic, and what started as an argument morphed into a genuine conversation. I meant to send him a copy of the strip, but by the time I'd gotten around to it he'd been fired himself.

AT LONG LAST SC PLUS PA

June 7, 2000 That Protoss is still on my desk, no lie. Trying to differentiate a frightening extraterrestrial from a common monster is a good deal more difficult that you'd think, especially when the person you are striving to convince really couldn't give a fuck one way or the other.

THE DEARLY DEPARTED

June 12, 2000 Yes, yes—Dreamcast, Dreamcast, Dreamcast. Look at Gabe's Goddamn hair! That's some zero-g type shit he is rocking there.

Funny Comes From Special Cows

These hilarious cows are the world's biggest source of funny. In fact, if you were to add up all the funny produced in a single year, it would be a lot - and I'm being totally serious! In the figure below, you can see all the awful stuff churning inside these merry beasts.

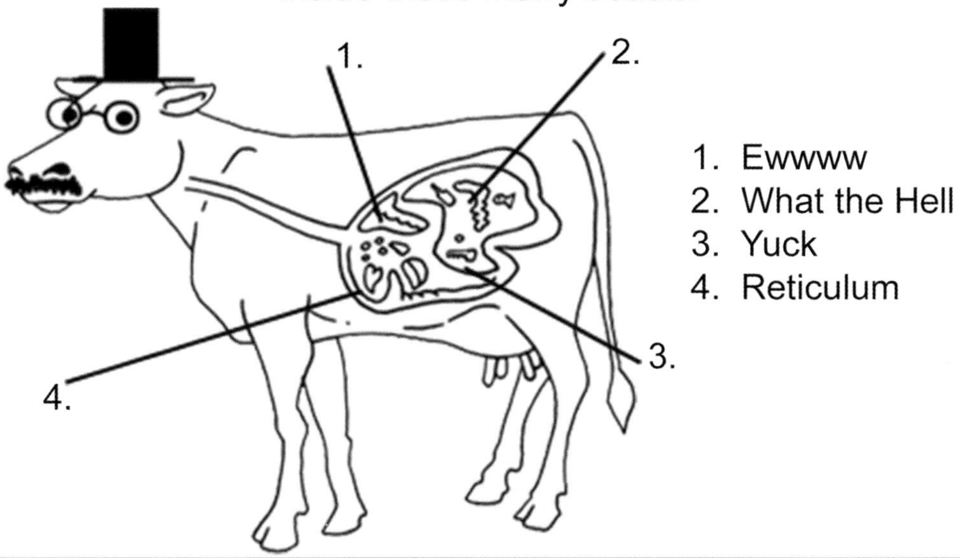

1. Ewwww
2. What the Hell
3. Yuck
4. Reticulum

WHERE DOES FUNNY COME FROM? PART 1

June 9, 2000 We saw a dairy council brochure online, and inspiration struck. Struck us *in* the head, actually. Struck us over and over in the head until, delirious, we made *this*. It turns out there's weird stuff in them cows.

Factory Fresh?
You Can Cownt On It

The cows, helpless to resist the machinations of the modern milking apparatus, now deliver the precious funny in record time. The humorless tanker drivers are sadly resigned to their grim destiny - to ferry funny to and fro, never themselves partaking of its richness, it's freshness.

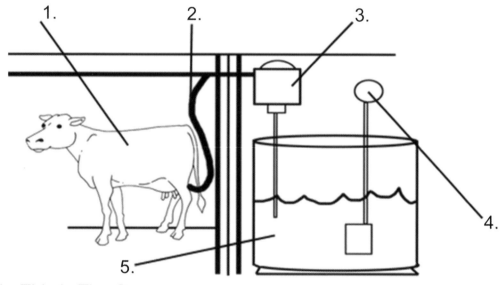

1. This Is The Cow
2. The Funny Goes Through Here
3. Then it has to Go In This Thing
4. Okay Now It's In The Other Thing
5. I Don't Know What That Is, An Oar Maybe

WHERE DOES FUNNY COME FROM? PART 2

June 9, 2000 Man, that tanker driver shit be ironic for *reals*.

Are You Like Blind
Or Something

I hear you asking yourselves, "Wait! But how does the funny get into my comics?" And I'm all, "Were these people dropped as babies? Am I the only one who sees this massive, important-looking machine?"

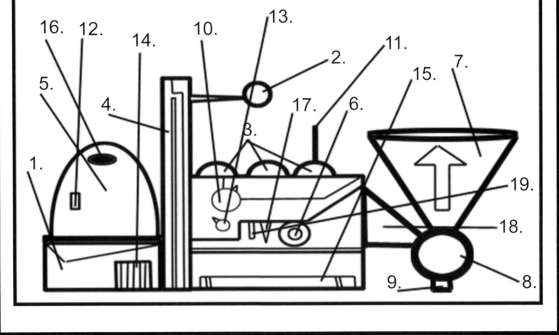

WHERE DOES FUNNY COME FROM? PART 3

June 9, 2000 This diagram is self-explanatory.

From Our Glands
To Your Hands

Mmmm... That's good! And as you can see
from this impish, contemptible face, more
funny means *more flavor!* Eat that sandwich,
you little bastard - eat it up! Maybe you'll choke and die!

WHERE DOES FUNNY COME FROM? PART 4

June 9, 2000 Then it gets weird.

Did you know?

In the 1600s, Europeans froze mixtures of funny, fruit and spices with a combination of ice, snow and saltpeter. These were probably the very first comic strips.

Watch Out

Not all comics use real funny! Look for this seal.

WHERE DOES FUNNY COME FROM? PART 5

June 9, 2000 Oh, I get it. That's actually a seal there. So it's like you're looking for a seal, which is actually a *seal*.

WILL WORK FOR GAMES

June 14, 2000 They *spring* that shit on you, and before you know it you've made some money choices that don't reflect well on your resolve. Before we understood that these companies were simply trying to pad the end of each quarter, we thought that we were just the playthings of some capricious gaming deity.

0 FOR 2

June 16, 2000 Every Goddamn person pronounces this word differently, and everyone is insufferable about it. Men have *died* trying to find the truth of it. I don't care anymore. I think the world can withstand a little mystery.

BOB, WE HARDLY KNEW YE

June 19, 2000 It struck a blow to Mac gamers, for whom good news was often rare—but Microsoft needed Halo, still does, and those motherfuckers can write a check so big it sounds like a brick when it hits the table.

PART ONE: NOT OSHA APPROVED

June 21, 2000 Speaking of Mac gamers, they were starting to get the major releases—and what's more, they were writing in with an eloquence and enthusiasm for my own pastime that made me reevaluate Chuck, a.k.a. "The ChuckzOr."

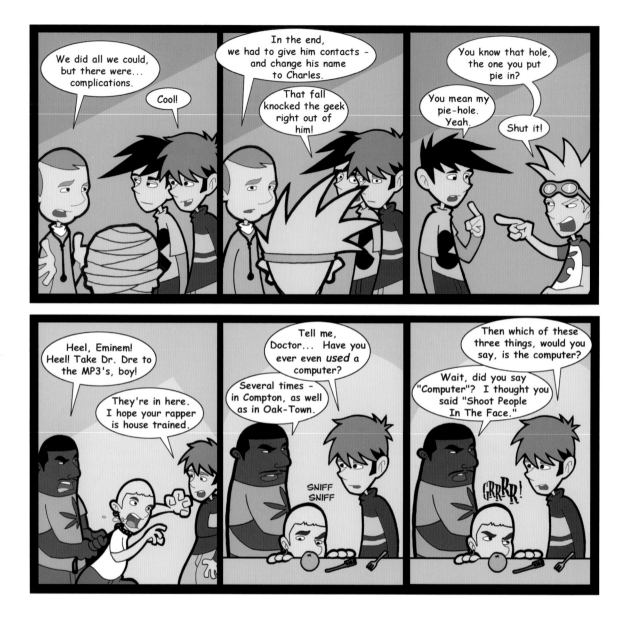

PART TWO: REBIRTH

June 23, 2000 I couldn't imagine why we needed some stupid cipher to represent Mac enthusiasts when it was becoming increasingly clear that they were, in fact, gamers—they simply had a more attractive system shell. So, we fixed it.

I FORGOT ABOUT DRE

June 26, 2000 It always seemed like if you could just sit Industry Entity X down for a little while and talk about how file sharing actually affects their business, you could effect some progress-oriented change. You might have to pull some *Mission: Impossible* shit to gain access to their fortified bunker, though.

PART ONE: ENTER THE DUMBASS

June 28, 2000 Gabe *did* like Draconus: Cult of the Wyrm, but let's be honest: this had nothing to do with Draconus or Cults, let *alone* Wyrms. It was basically about kicking *Daily Radar* in the balls, over and over.

PART TWO: DOUBLE SHOT

June 30, 2000 The evil Scott Kurtz had just completed a storyline where two of his characters were stuck in an elevator for two weeks, which *we* then referenced. I, um . . . It seemed like a good idea at the time.

PART THREE: HA-HA-HA!

July 3, 2000 The shocking conclusion! Take that, game news website! We certainly showed you not to, well, do the jobs that you get paid to do, I guess. Anyway, you were *shown!*

DO YOU LIKE PINA COLADAS?

July 5, 2000 Warren Spector worked at Looking Glass, which we eulogized earlier in this volume. He also recorded a couple albums under the pseudonym "Warren G," jumpstarting the genre known as "G-Funk."

JUST LIKE YOUR REMEMBER

July 7, 2000 This is another comic which is sometimes acted out in front of us. We might sell a *shirt* for example, and with a grin the young man we've just made a transaction with will jam the garment into his shorts.

SOME LIKE IT MOIST

July 10, 2000 This is the first strip Gabe ever drew with the Wacom tablet. Like a wild animal, he wasn't sure to what extent he could trust this wily device. Eventually, he came up with the system he still uses: draw on paper, and then scan it in for finish work.

SONY ARCADE

July 12, 2000 This strip was actually accompanied by a quick and dirty redesign of the site to better establish Sony's new dominance of our output.

BUT THAT'S THE BEST PART

July 14, 2000 We'd read an article in *GameFan* about this new law, and immediately began to fantasize about the kind of erotic arcade such games would find a home in. Sometimes, on a rainy day, I'll see that arcade in my mind's eye and smile.

RED AND BLUE IN: THE PARTY

July 17, 2000 We used the concept a few more times, but I don't know if they were ever any better than this one.

TIPS FROM THE PROS

July 19, 2000 We'd gotten hooked on Sega's Virtua Tennis, to the extent that we were actually inviting over human beings and incorporating it into a kind of party atmosphere. O Sega, wherefore art thou?

CULTURAL REFERENCES 'R US

July 21, 2000 It must be said: Kool-Aid is one of the most delicious fluids on the planet. When we started the site, we'd drink a pitcher a day at least, double sugar. Man-O-Mango powered the lion's share of this collection.

I HAVEN'T SLEPT IN THREE DAYS

July 24, 2000 This cartoon is pretty insane, but I had some kind of tooth problem that would pulse agony through my entire jaw, robbing me of restful sleep. In my delirium, I somehow convinced myself that Tribes 2 was responsible.

SEGA, WHY HAST THOU FORSAKEN ME?

July 26, 2000 I'm not saying that we're the best people in the world to judge a baseball game or anything, but I'm not entirely sure what game they were trying to simulate. Between each inning—a period of time the game calls a "Hargir"—gaunt spirits emerge to harvest living flesh.

THIS IS A POLITICAL CARTOON

July 28, 2000 These days, we have a lobotomized version of Napster through which we can purchase legitimate songs under the watchful eye of Lars Ulrich. He knows what songs you buy, and if they are not sufficiently hardcore, he broods in the darkness from his onyx throne.

REGISTER THIS

July 31, 2000 Before everyone realized that the Internet was just a series of computers connected to each other and not an eternal, emerald fairyland of leprechaun gold, they were trying to tell you that registering a domain was going to be the defining moment of your life. It's actually true, in my case, but I'd never give them the satisfaction.

BACK BY POPULAR DEMAND

August 2, 2000 There was a ton of Mac news that needed tellin', Mac readers pressured us into it, we liked Charles, and so then you had this. In the same way that scissors is able to defeat paper, we've always thought of Charles as emitting a kind of anti-Gabe *force*.

I'LL JUST PUT THIS RIGHT HERE

August 7, 2000 We were so happy that someone was paying us to run *Penny Arcade* that we didn't read the contract very thoroughly. It turns out we'd actually sold the site, and the money we were getting was just payments on the purchase price. Whoops! They could do anything they wanted to your page, which inspired this comic.

SON OF TOO DAMN LATE

August 4, 2000 I don't know what more you could possibly want in a comic strip. It's got *fish*, you know, it's got, like . . . *marine* biologists, and those are cool. Punch it with muscle relaxants, and you're golden. Next!

G AND T IN: DON'T EAT MY FEMUR

August 9, 2000 The comic itself is sort of bizarre and nonsensical, properties we're no stranger to, I guess. Though I always did enjoy this title. Typically, it's just *implied* that you'd prefer your femur remain uneaten.

RED AND BLUE IN DAYS OF OLD

August 11, 2000 I actually wanted to make a whole strip just about Red and Blue, and even these days I'm always trying to push Gabe in that direction. I've been trying for multiple years by this point, so I think the chances are pretty low. Plus, there's other guys doing it.

(CRASH OF THUNDER)

August 14, 2000 I've always really liked this comic, but I don't have any idea where it fits into the larger framework. Tycho, a man of science?

THAT'S A LOT OF POUNDS

August 16, 2000 I was really into Icewind Dale at the time. It was a game billed as being pure "hack und slash" but had a few really great story hooks. Gabriel was just getting into elaborate mechanisms, so this one just sort of wrote itself.

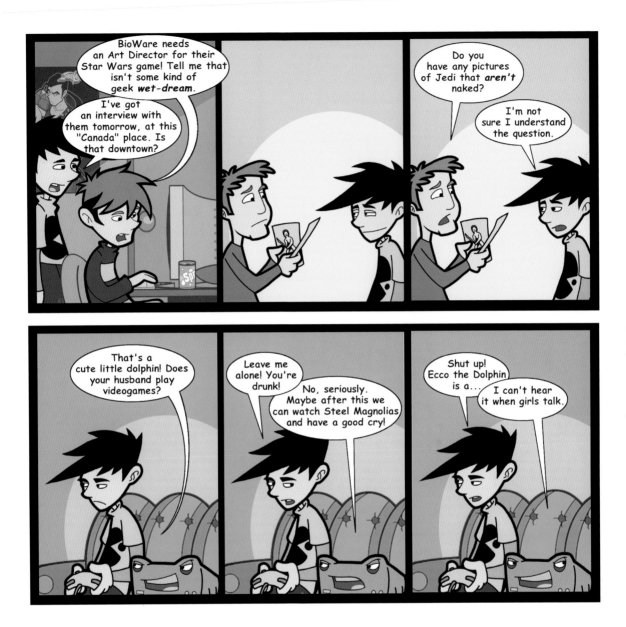

STAR WHORES

August 18, 2000 Clearly, Gabe trying to get on Game Developer X is another theme of which we've taken full advantage. I've seen the drawings referenced in this strip, and I think that by and large they do honor the Jedi tradition. By and large.

FEATURING DIV

August 20, 2000 Yes, Div is there, and he's being mean, because he represents the hypermas-culine impulse we strive to repress. Ecco the Dolphin, though—for the Dreamcast? Holy *shit*. This game had us by the *balls*. Which we totally have, even if we play games with dolphins in them.

WE'RE VERY, VERY SORRY

August 23, 2000 This still happens, actually—there are just games that we miss—and the violence with which the fact is enunciated by the readership is intense. I don't know how you would measure the intense heat of their loathing. Could any human thermometer withstand it?

PA: THROUGH THE YEARS

August 25, 2000 In the post that accompanies this strip on the site, we urged readers to be cautiously enthusiastic about Nintendo's Gamecube, a policy which the passage of time has borne out. Like the Nintendo 64 before it, the machine had a series of absolutely genre-defining, *must-play* titles.

I've always wished I could endorse the machine with unmitigated vigor, because I support Nintendo's basic philosophy: that videogames are a potent medium, one that anyone should be able to enjoy. This utterly confounds the hardcore player, because—unlike the rest of the entire Goddamn industry—every move of the company isn't catered to their petulant whim.

ADVANCED GAMING STUDIES (AGS)

August 28, 2000 Our bold program was eventually shut down in a spectacular F.B.I. raid.

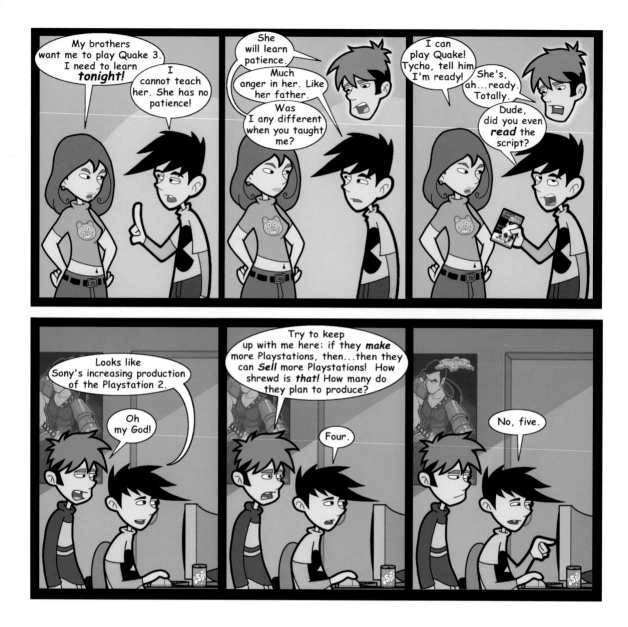

WILL SHE COMPLETE THE TRAINING?

August 30, 2000 Kara might not have been what we think of as a gamer originally, but after her brother got her into it she just never got back out. She has a lot of natural talent that might otherwise have been squandered on useful endeavors.

"CREATING DEMAND" BY SONY

September 4, 2000 And, wouldn't you know it, there weren't enough on launch day, and they got their media shots of gamers outside, after midnight, in the middle of winter. Our dedication to these machines is actually somewhat maniacal.

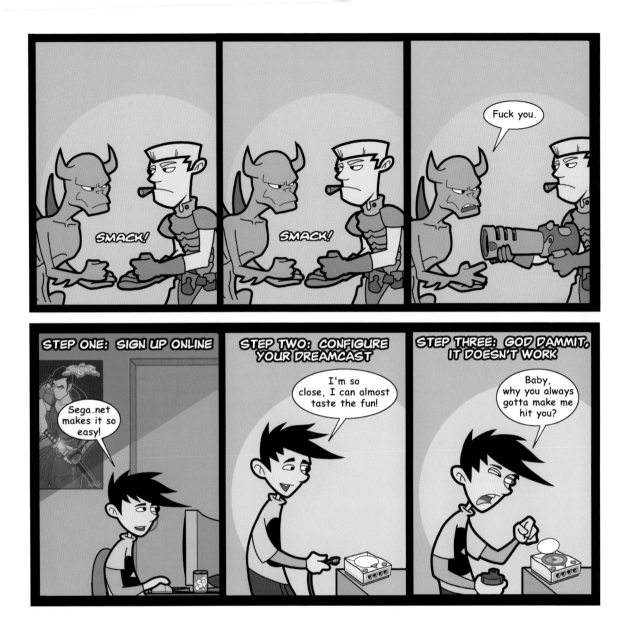

RPS

September 5, 2000 Even while we played the other games that came out, we always got together every night on Sidewinder GameVoice and played one of the Capture The Flag variants for Quake 3. So *satisfying*. These characters are the Quake 3 versions of Red and Blue.

SEGA.NET: IT DOESN'T WORK™

September 8, 2000 It's hard to believe how ahead of the curve Sega was putting Internet capable games in the living room. Not just the old PC genres that had already gotten the treatment, either—mass market sports titles, goofy action experiences, mouse herding . . . Fucking multi-player mouse herding!

CHOOSE . . . BUT CHOOSE WISELY

September 11, 2000 When The Lamb of Hosts shows up in PA, we'll get angry mail from one or two people. If we say something unkind about a *gaming platform*, like "Xbox controllers are *big*," we get hundreds upon hundreds of mails. I don't know if our culture is sick or what.

PART ONE: CONFRONTATION

September 13, 2000 This is the first part of a Div storyline. You might notice that I am drawn here as a *radish*. Gabriel threatened to draw me thus for as long as I held out on buying a Dreamcast, a threat I didn't take seriously. Clearly, I underestimated the man.

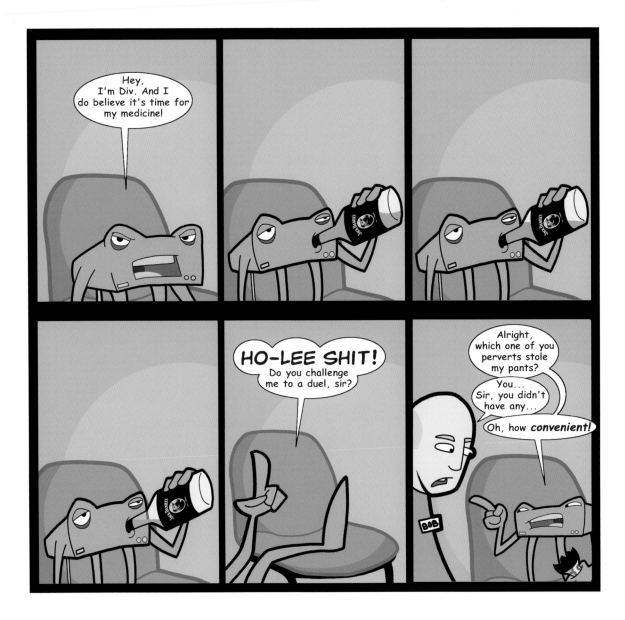

PART TWO: RESOLUTION

September 15, 2000 Div drinks! *Check it out.*

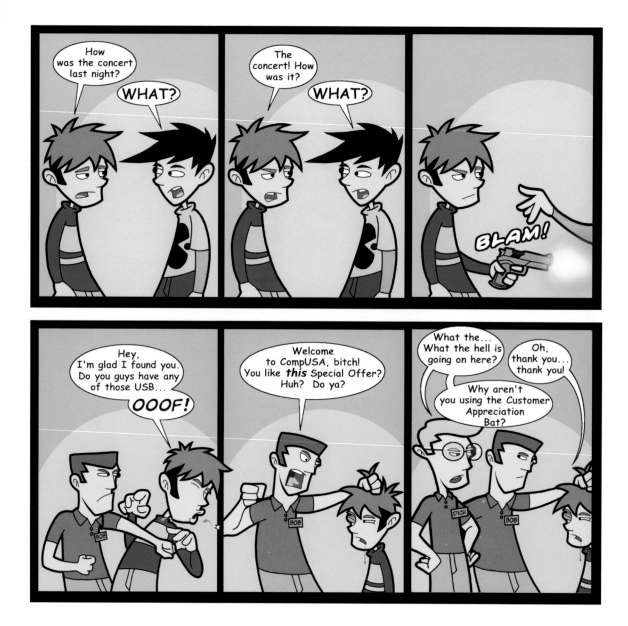

THANK YOU, DRIVE THROUGH

September 18, 2000 I'm sure there's a lesson here, I'm not sure exactly what it is. If I ask you how a concert was though, you know, hook a brother up. Otherwise, I'm bound to get handy with the steel.

TRUE STORY

September 20, 2000 Sometimes people will bring us bats to sign, a process that somehow christens them as Customer Appreciation Bats. Seen from a distance, it looks like they're coming over to start some *shit*. So those first few exchanges are always uneasy.

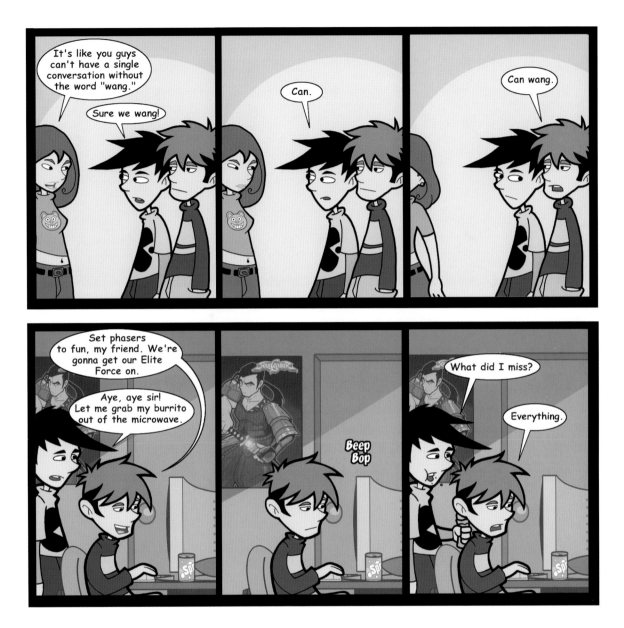

RHYMES WITH TANG

September 22, 2000 "Wang" is now a kind of rallying cry for a certain sort of *Penny Arcade* reader. There's a World of Warcraft guild called "Keepers of the Wang." When a link from the site cripples a server, that equipment is said to have been "Wanged." I came up with a fancier term for it, a *classier* term, one that did not reference cocks. It never stuck.

ELITE FARCE

September 25, 2000 We loved *Elite Force*, as long as it lasted anyway. At nine total hours, there just wasn't much there to hate.

WHY, GOD, WHY?

September 27, 2000 Tribes 2 wasn't "rushed out the door" so much as "dragged to the door by men twice its size and hurled bodily *from* it." Dynamix had great ideas, some embraced by the community and some not, but in the end the almost weekly patches made us hang it up.

ONE PART SWASH, TWO PARTS BUCKLE

September 29, 2000 Mechwarrior and Crimson Skies have both had console iterations by this point, and where the Xbox versions tend toward accessibility, the PC versions always veered dangerously close to sim. I say dangerously, but I always relished them. Taking fantasy very seriously is sort of my thing.

SUIT DAEMONS, PART VI

October 2, 2000 Things continued to go south for sites tricked into joining advertising collectives, as we had done. This time it was Express.com, which had collected many notable sites of that time period. I don't recall exactly, but I *believe* the person depicted in the strip is Lowtax of Something Awful fame.

AND FOR MY NEXT TRICK

October 4, 2000 If you start to sing the theme from Sega's Daytona racer, and all you get is *killed*, you probably got off lucky.

NEWS YOU CAN USE

October 6, 2000 Here is the newscaster who would eventually be named "Randy," which is clearly appropriate. I didn't remember that he'd started as a symbol of the media's ineptitude where electronic entertainment is concerned. These days, we produce him when we need to touch on multiple topics in a single strip.

AN OFFICIAL ACCIDENT

October 11, 2000 Someone had created some fairly erotic Everquest fanfic, posted it somewhere on the net, and it started a chain of events that culminated in the player being banned from the game. I'm told that the Vah Shir cat-men still yowl in nightly vigils for this stalwart, sensual hero.

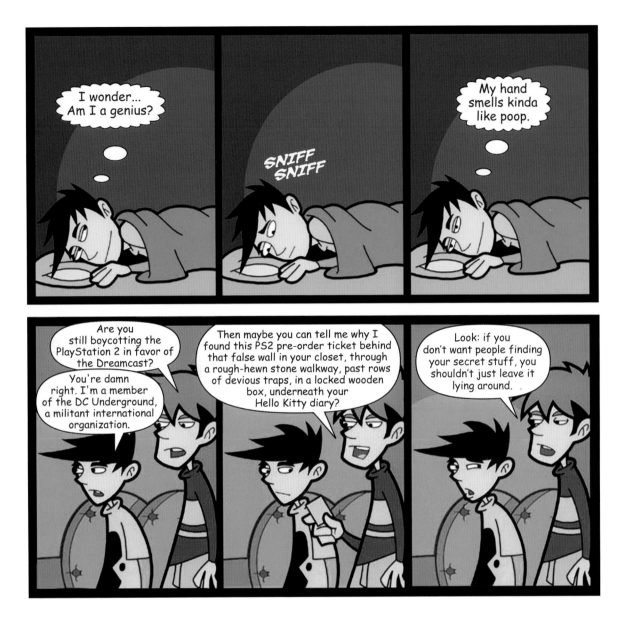

I WOULDN'T SAY "GENIUS," EXACTLY

October 13, 2000 Gabriel assures me that this is a true story.

. . . A REVELATION

October 16, 2000 Even with his frenzied ardor for the Dreamcast, he wasn't able to resist the call of a new system. At a fundamental level we just like *games*, and the idea that some portion of them would be inaccessible is almost unthinkable.

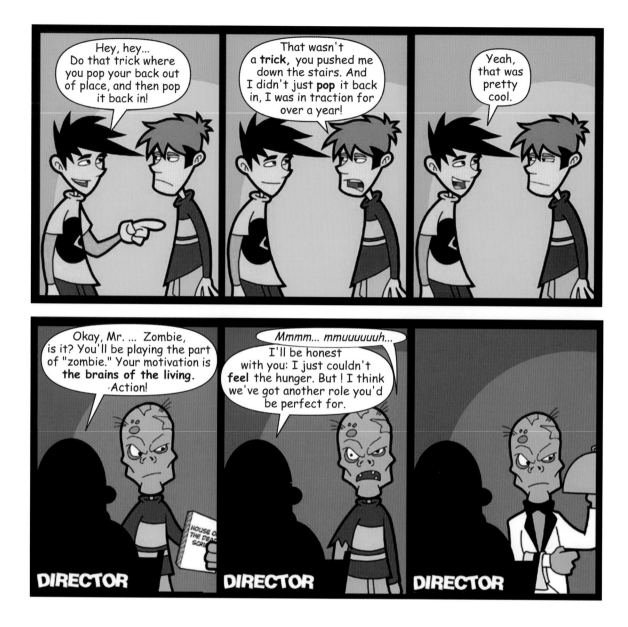

ONE-TRICK TYCHO

October 18, 2000 There is a lot to learn in this strip, about, you know . . . *Spines*. Shit be *educational*.

AUDITIONS OF THE DAMNED

October 20, 2000 Before we had any idea who Uwe Boll was—Uwe Boll, who we now know to be an infamous brand molester—we were already afraid of what he'd do with House of the Dead. And I won't rest until the man stands trial before an international body for his crimes against *eyes*.

IT IS ALSO CALLED "MOOLAH"

October 23, 2000 Oddworld Inhabitants' Lorne Lanning has become a kind of maniacal figure in *Penny Arcade* lore. He's recently given up the games industry for good, with the idea of making television shows for China. Or something. I didn't really understand what he was talking about.

THAT'S GOTTA HURT

October 27, 2000 We got a lot of mail about this one, asking what the symbolism of the whole thing was, but the reality was we thought it'd be funny to see a man kicked in the face by a horse and, being so kicked, exclaim "Orff."

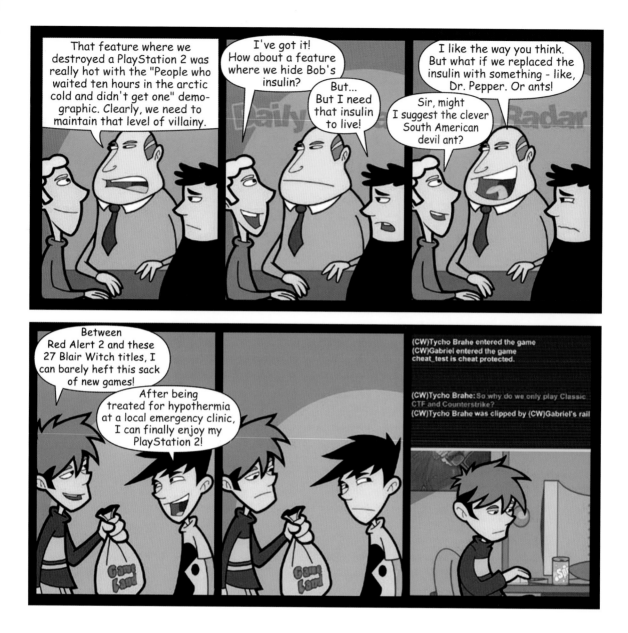

THEY'VE GOT LITTLE HORNS

October 30, 2000 Tensions remained high with *Daily Radar*, as you can see. They really did destroy a PS2. They said that it didn't work anymore, but they were base liars all. Deceit was their stock in trade.

THERE ARE ONLY TWO REAL GAMES

November 1, 2000 It's actually kind of a relief to have a nightly game your whole crew is fixated on. You can play any other game that comes out and see the best in it, because your real investment is elsewhere.

I THINK WE GOT EVERYBODY

November 3, 2000 Never let it be said that we do not endeavor to satisfy you completely! Except when we don't! In those cases, you are free to say that.

THIS ISN'T THE FIRST TIME

November 6, 2000 We were playing a lot of Sega's Jet Grind Radio at the time. It was a good game, to be sure, but Gabriel's hands had somehow fused to the Dreamcast controller which severely limited both his mobility *and* the available titles.

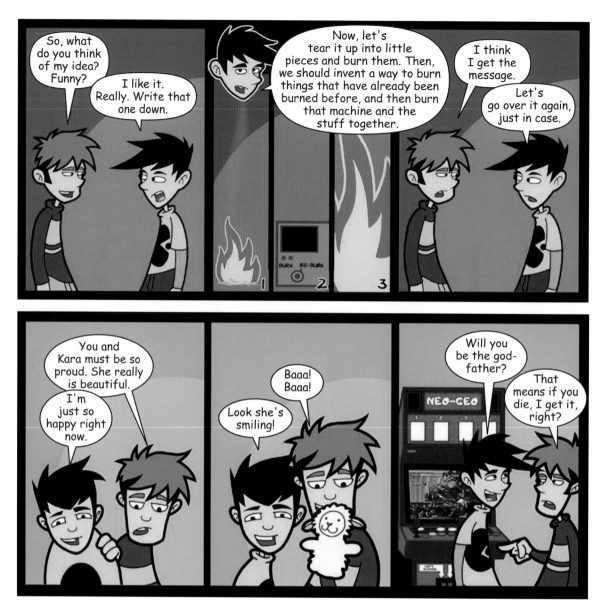

THE ONES YOU LOVE

November 8, 2000 I don't know how two implacable egotists are able to agree on anything, but we've managed to work together on projects of varying kinds for coming up on twelve years. Brenna's theory is that we are actually one person, partitioned in the moment before beingness. Okay, I made that up.

PAPA'S GOING TO BUY YOU

November 10, 2000 "The Corner Arcade" as an idea has atrophied to a terrific extent, and this decline made a four slot Neo Geo cabinet available to him for just *three hundred dollars*. The idea of owning an arcade machine was opulence beyond reckoning, on par with owning a golden, time-traveling rhinoceros.

"GOLD" IS A EUPHEMISM

November 13, 2000 Gabe had just read Michael Crichton's *Timeline*, which let me know to avoid it—but when a game based on it hit stores, we decided we might as well grab it. Reviews had been conspicuously absent, and we'd soon learn why: the game, the *entire* game, was twenty minutes long.

SHENMUE: WOW!

November 15, 2000 For somebody supposedly overwrought about the death of his father, magic artifacts, and his family's *dark* secrets, Ryo Hazaki spends a lot of time hanging out and screwing around. It was my favorite game for a very long time, so I guess it didn't bother me too much.

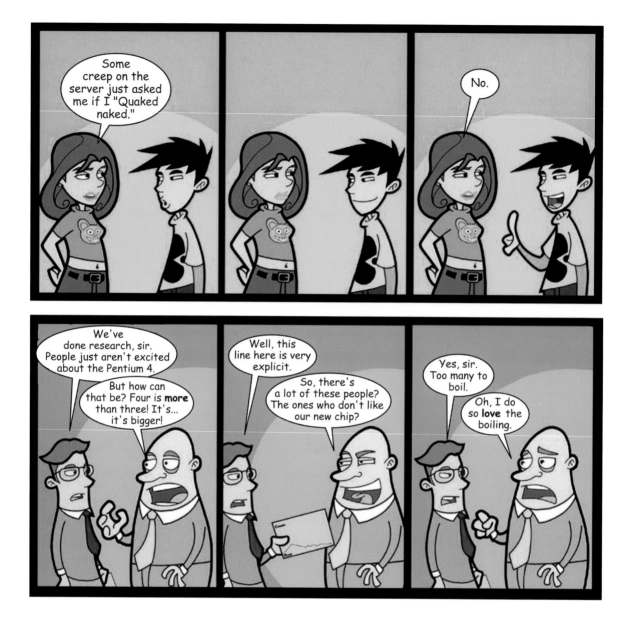

PRETTY PLEASE

November 17, 2000 Kara's handle then was Angel Eyes, which caught her no end of harassment when she'd throw down online. Eventually, her skill with the rocket launcher and aerial shots would earn her a new handle: Orbital Strike.

OH BOY, CAN'T WAIT

November 20, 2000 The days where I would slaver in anticipation over some new processor, churning through site after site for graphs of varying kinds have been over for a while. I care about new hardware these days to the extent that it makes my transit into digital realms more complete. Before this strip, it was an end in itself.

AN IMPORTANT BULLETIN

November 21, 2000 Oh, we tease you because we love you. Also: your misery is *delicious!*

MAYBE THEY'RE HIDING

November 24, 2000 You know how it is when you get sent for something, but to get it you need to walk by the computer, and if you're by the computer anyway why don't you just check your Hotmail, oh hey look, Bob is on AIM . . .

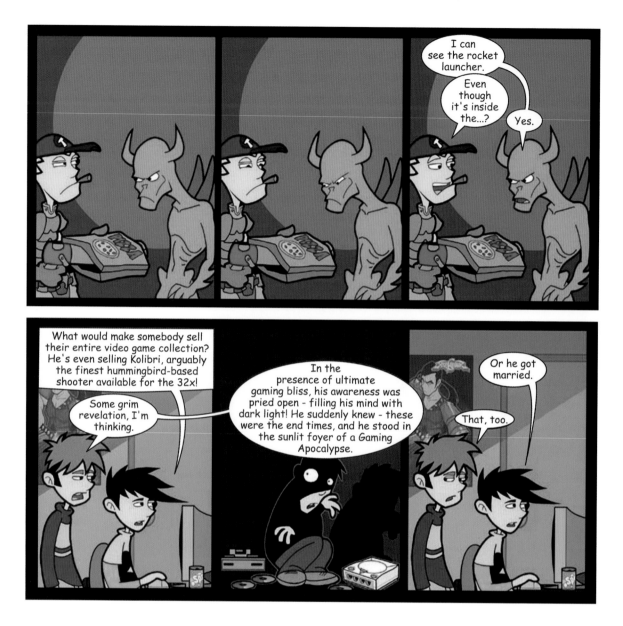

RED & BLUE IN . . . WE DELIVER

November 27, 2000 For years, whenever anyone would ask me what my favorite *Penny Arcade* strip was, I would refer them to this one. I thought Gabe handled the alien weirdo's frustration really well.

I MUST NOT RECALL

November 29, 2000 This was the first huge collection we'd ever seen auctioned off, and it was a truly mouthwatering array. We'd go over to eBay to read that list and watch the high bid crawl toward the stratosphere.

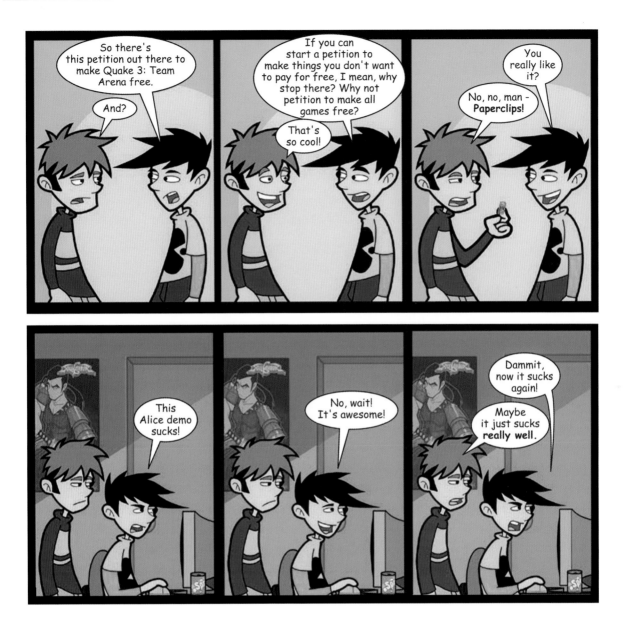

QUAKE 3: FREE ARENA

December 1, 2000 Epic gives away tons of UT content in the form of its various Map Packs, content which is of uniformly high quality. They'd never given away anything as rich as the additions in Quake 3: Team Arena, of course, but the paradigm had already shifted. As paradigms are wont to do.

SEE ALICE JUMP

December 4, 2000 The next time we would make fun of American McGee's X, where X equals whatever he was doing, we'd end up in huge legal trouble—but that's a story for later. Did he use evil magic to create turbulence in our lives? This is what I secretly believe.

PEELANCER

December 6, 2000 The game eventually delivered as Freelancer was pretty good, I thought—different than I expected, but, as I established earlier in the book, I'll take my Space Sims however I can get them. The multi let you host an entire universe and play with friends, which was hot to death.

AH, THE CLASSICS!

December 8, 2000 Man, *seriously* though. That Optimus Prime shit was ice cold. Please, God—tell me that the people reading this book know what I'm talking about. Please don't let me be really, really *old*.

WHAT IS WRONG WITH ME?

December 11, 2000 One thing you can say for the *Tomb Raider* movie is that it didn't directly scar the retina. Certainly the trailer caused no serious injury. And trust me, we would know.

'TIS THE SEASON

December 13, 2000 Ah, to be young again! With a porous conscience and a knack for explosive devices!

EVEN PA HAS LIMITS

December 15, 2000 When I lament the squandered momentum of the PlayStation Portable, I often forget—until my own ancient comics remind me—that the PlayStation 2 itself didn't always stand astride the world.

ACTUALLY, IT WAS

December 18, 2000 This is the comic where Gabriel and Div throw a brick at Tycho. For some reason. It's never really gone into.

THINK "ONI"

December 20, 2000 This is the most sensible answer to The Box Question I've read anywhere.

I MEAN, WHO DOESN'T?

December 22, 2000 The days when you could do your Christmas shopping exclusively at CompUSA were what I would call *good* days. These days it's all candle stores in the mall and *The Bon Marche* and despair.

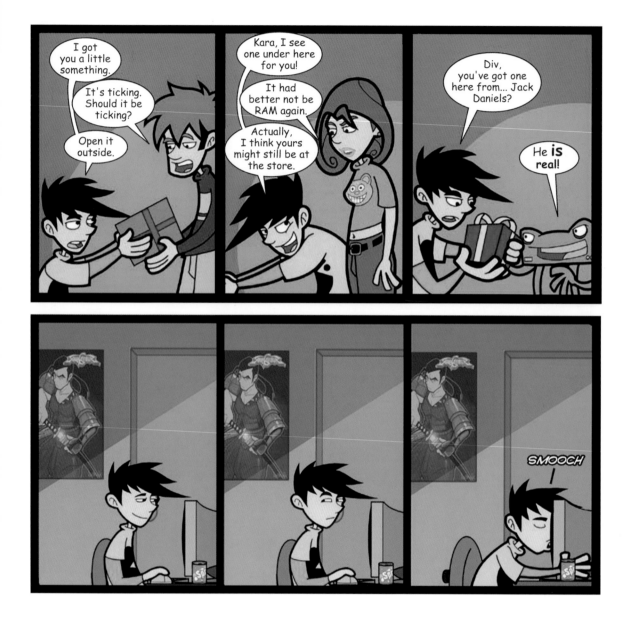

MERRY FUCKING CHRISTMAS

December 25, 2000 I always really liked the punch on this one, even years later. Lord only knows how long Div had written to that Tennessee distillery without reply. Providing wish fulfillment for characters you invented yourself is really satisfying for some reason.

NO ONE NEEDS TO KNOW

December 27, 2000 Hey, listen—whatever you want to do with your computer in a dimly lit room is your thing. Just, you know, make sure the webcam is off. That's all we're asking.

Dear Fuckers,

I rue the day I purchased your Cleanmates monitor wipes. I also rue when I used the wipes themselves. Even throwing the whole thing in the garbage was a hassle, though I don't know that I rued it per se.

"Quick-Dry, Non-Streaking Formula" my ass. Now I have to buy new wipes to clean off the shit your stupid ones left on my screen.

I Hate You Guys,

Michael Krahulik
"Gabriel"

p.s. I just rued again.

Are you sure you used the wipes correctly?

I took them out of the thingy, and then I moved them back and forth on my monitor.

Fair enough.

RUE, RUE, RUE YOUR BOAT

December 29, 2000 The product was called CleanMates' Non-Streak Wipes, and virtually every word of their name is a lie. They're oily, they aren't your friend, and they *do* leave streaks—streaks of opaque grease on everything they touch. So you *could* wipe something with them, but really, I mean . . . Why would you?

The Webcomic Manifesto

Typically when people discuss the "ramifications" of Webcomics (capital W, proper noun) the discussion adopts a kind of revolutionary tone. The more serious proponents of the medium think of the mysterious Internet as a means by which the yoke of oppression may be cast off. Or something. As a person who never saw their creative output in the context of domination to begin with, the metaphor never sat right.

In any case, the dialogue tends to focus on how digital distribution of comics alters the power dynamic between creators and publishers.

I guess so.

The most startling change we've seen hasn't been between creators and publishers, it's between creators and readers. I understand why the story doesn't get told, because there are no great dragons in it, slain by the rough sword of the common man. This movie will not be directed by Jerry Bruckheimer. However, as it's completely reconfigured my life, I thought I'd mention it.

I'm talking about a system of distribution where the creator says to the reader "Here is everything I have ever made. It is yours, free, for as long as you want it."

Most of the people considered "big movers" in Webcomics are considered so not because they have substantially contributed work to the medium—indeed, they might not even produce a regularly updated comic. No, they are thought of with reverence because in each case they laud some new barrier between people who read comics and people who write them. The barriers they're so proud of take a number of forms, but Byzantine pay mechanisms and subscription-locked archives are two of the more celebrated anchors.

If you are using systems like these, I need to ask you why you don't trust your readers.

What are you afraid they're going to do with your comics? Read them?

Readers will take care of you. I'm speaking from personal experience. They won't rest; they'll invent a way to do it. And if you aren't meeting them halfway, your archives open, if you are not inviting a person into your work, I'm prepared to say that you aren't making Webcomics.

In fact, if you're standing in front of the fucking Internet with your arms folded until somebody pays up, I don't know what to call that. You're playing at business. I think you brought your odd hierarchies, your paranoia, and your publishing-as-usual cynicism into the only medium that allows true parity with creators.

It may be that you're happy with a subset of a subset of the people who actually give a fuck about comics, online or off. By all means, continue to languish. When you're ready to stop treating readers like thieves, come check out this Web they've got going. I hear it's going to be big.